FRAGMENTS OF HISTORY
THE ESSAYS BEHIND THE STORIES
BY AMRA PAJALIC

∞

MELBOURNE, AUSTRALIA

https://www.pishukinpress.com/

Copyright © 2025 by Amra Pajalić

First Published 2025

Pishukin Press

All rights reserved. This book is copyright. Apart from fair dealing for the purpose of private study, research, criticism or review, as permitted under the copyright act, no part may be reproduced by any process without written permission from author.

Cover design: Created using Canva elements, image attribution Photo by AdnanV via Dreamstime

For content and trigger warnings please go towww.amrapajalic.com/themes

Quality control: We care about producing error-free books. If you discover a typo or formatting issue, please contact admin@pishukinpress.com

Paperback Edition: 9781922871565

Contents

1. Introduction — 1
2. Srebrenica as a symbol — 4
3. The Siege Begins: Survival in Srebrenica — 26
4. The Urban / Rural Divide in Yugoslavia — 51
5. Bosnia as a pluralist society — 69
6. The role of intermarriage within what was Yugoslavia — 81
7. Women in war — 88
8. Conclusion — 110
9. Handout: Organisations and Resources to Learn More About Srebrenica — 113
10. Bibliography — 116

Glossary — 123

Seka Torlak Series — 127

About the author — 131

Also by — 134

Introduction

My novel *Time Kneels Between Mountains*, is a blend of historical fiction and murder mystery, bringing to life one of the most devastating and underrepresented chapters in modern history: the Srebrenica genocide.

Set against the backdrop of Srebrenica during the Bosnian War, *Time Kneels Between Mountains* plunges readers into a small-town mystery brimming with intrigue, betrayal, and forbidden love.

On July 11, 1995, Serbian forces in Srebrenica, Bosnia and Herzegovina, killed 8,372 men and boys, burying them in mass graves; this made it the biggest massacre in Europe since World War II.

The Srebrenica massacre led to the unanimous ruling the massacre of the enclave's male inhabitants constituted genocide, a crime under international law, in 2004 in the case of Prosecutor v. Krstić in the Appeals Chamber of the ICTY (Prosecutor v. Krstić, Case No. IT-98-33-A, 2004).

As a result, this event is historically significant, as it is the first genocide conviction in Europe since the Holocaust. It is a globally significant event as it represents the catastrophic failure of the international community to prevent genocide, despite numerous warnings.

Through its historical setting and layered characters, the novel sheds light on the human toll of war while exploring themes of identity, memory, and justice. Srebrenica, an enclave that became the site of genocide during the war, serves as both the setting and the heart of the story.

As a Bosnian author, I draw on my heritage to craft an own voices narrative that brings authenticity and sensitivity to this harrowing topic. I completed this novel as the creative component of my PhD in Creative Writing thesis, examining the role of historical fiction in preserving and interpreting memories of the Bosnian Genocide.

I have developed teaching resources based on this research with information sheets and essays that can support learning about war, remembrance, and persecution.

By broadening the scope to include the Bosnian Genocide, I aim to provide students with a more comprehensive understanding of genocide studies, encouraging critical reflection on global history and human rights.

My intention is to create historical essays showcasing the narrative of what happened within Srebrenica and examine the various factors that contributed to the massacre, highlight underrepresented stories within this historical event, and more importantly, showcase the ingenuity and resilience of the people of Srebrenica who endured this siege.

I hope readers will learn about these events, can think more critically about the role of discrimination and prejudice in dehumanising people and creating division in society.

I have drawn on excellent academic research in developing these essays, and strongly encourage readers to continue their exploration by reading the primary sources. I have created and freely shared these essays to foster learning and advocacy.

I hope to continue my work in advocating and sharing lessons about Srebrenica in the future and if you would like to be a part of this journey, please connect with me.

Amra Pajalic

Srebrenica as a symbol

My argument that Srebrenica is a historically significant event is based on the concept of memorialisation as an essential function of historical novels. De Groot (2009) states that "novels have quite an odd historiography, continually suggesting that history is something which happens despite the actions of the individual but simultaneously celebrating the historically significant actions of that individual" (p. 83). This reflects the tension in historical fiction, where history seems to unfold beyond the control of individual actions, yet those same actions are highlighted as being historically significant.

My research represents specific historical perspectives and narratives of Bosnian identity within the context of the Srebrenica siege. As a Bosnian who lived through the communist era as a child in 1985-1989, I bring a particular lens to this interrogation. My lived experience informs my understanding of the complex and evolving nature of Bosnian identity during this period, which is vastly different from the identity of contemporary Bosnia. This thesis is also my opportunity to integrate the history of my people and the genocide within my writing to better connect with my culture.

In doing so, this research contributes to an increased and nuanced understanding of this conflict. Hikmet Karčić and Richard Newell (2023) argue that there is a need for "the continued study of the genocide" because there is "a real lack of awareness about the Bosnian

Genocide," consequently, we need "better education" (p. 25). Bosnian Genocide Studies explores the genocide through "the continued study of its roots, preparation, execution, and lingering aftermath" (Karčić and Newell 2023, p. 21). I hope that through my novel and thesis, as well as these essays, I contribute to the area of Bosnian Studies and "help bring Bosnian scholarship to a wide audience and ensure that voices of Bosnian (diaspora) scholars are heard" (Karčić and Newell 2023, p. 35).

This interrogation is essential, as historical novels are intricately involved in shaping the historical memory of Srebrenica. They contribute to how both current and future generations conceptualise the genocide and engage with broader questions of Bosnian identity. I argue that novels about Srebrenica are historical novels because this process of memorialisation is an essential function of this genre. In doing so, I deploy historian Pierre Nora's theory of *lieux de mémoire* (Nora 1989, p. 7), a French term that means sites of memory, and argue that Srebrenica is a symbol of a collective memory where the cultural and national memory of what was Yugoslavia is preserved, commemorated and transformed.

Stijn Vervaet (2011), in his study *Writing War, Writing Memory*, builds upon the theoretical foundations of collective memory developed by Jan and Aleida Assmann. The Assmanns, in turn, draw on the work of French sociologist Maurice Halbwachs, who conceptualised memory as a "social product" (Assmann 1992, as cited in Vervaet, p. 2). As such collective memory is "distinct from history and consisting of the cultural representations of a certain group living in a certain area" (Assmann 1992 as cited in Vervaet 2011, p. 2). Using this theory Srebrenica helps to keep the memory of an important historical event of the genocide alive and plays a crucial role in how Bosniaks understand and relate to their past.

Furthermore, Assmann notes that "collective memory changes over time," and "the memories of the group are formed in a fashion that allows them to be adjusted to contemporary ideas or presumptions and to the desires of the society" (Assmann 1992, 1999, as cited in Vervaet 2011, p. 3). When exploring Srebrenica and the way that collective memory has been constructed from before the war, during the war, and in the aftermath of the massacre we can see that the various political and ideological factors have influenced the collective memory.

Nora introduced the concept of *lieux de mémoire* in his work on how societies remember the past. He states that:

> Our interest in *lieux de memoire* where memory crystallises and secretes itself has occurred at a particular historical moment, a turning point where consciousness of a break with the past is bound up with the sense that memory has been torn—but torn in such a way as to pose the problem of the embodiment of memory in certain sites where a sense of historical continuity persists. There are *lieuxde memoire,* sites of memory, because there are no longer *milieux de memoire,* real environments of memory (Nora 1989, p. 7).

In applying Pierre Nora's concept of *lieuxde mémoire* (sites of memory) to Srebrenica the town's history and memory have been fractured by the genocide and transformed in the aftermath of the Bosnian War.

Srebrenica before the war demonstrates what Nora would describe as a *milieu de mémoire*—a real environment where memory was lived, organically maintained by the people and their interactions with the town and each other.

Srebrenica was named after the silver mines that had formed the backbone of its economy in the fourteenth century: *srebro* in Bosnian means silver and so Srebrenica literally translates to Silver City (Honig and Both 1996, p. xviii). Chuck Sudetic (1998) notes the "[f]ights in Srebrenica over its mineral health going on for centuries" (p. 139) and as the "[w]ealth pouring in from silver mines attracted kings and feudal strongmen" (p. 139). It became one of the largest mining centres and "its silver smelters were belching out so much soot and ash that the townspeople complained about air pollution" (Sudetic 1998, p. 139). In 1992, when the Balkan War commenced, its silver had been depleted for centuries, however, the city was still a well-developed "mineral-mining region before the war" (Sudetic 1998, p. 139).

Before the war, Srebrenicians gained a sense of identity from being Yugoslavs and the benefactors of the town's wealth as a mining town. Even though Yugoslavia was Communist by the 1990s, most residents of Srebrenica were living a very comfortable life that was equal to the United States and Western Europe, and "nearly every miner or factory worker had an apartment, car and summer cottage"(Rohde 2012, p. 7). This modern lifestyle came from Yugoslavia's Communist government's foresight in establishing factories that built car batteries and brakes, and the bauxite and zinc mines (Rohde 2012, p. iv). Sudetic (1998) notes that those who lived in town benefited the most from this new economic upturn and people "stopped taking note of who was a Muslim or who was a Serb" (p. 145).

Even though most of the memories of WWII were forgotten "outcroppings of the old enmities and the old jealousies surfaced during squabbles over who would be chosen to fill a sought-after job opening, which family would be allocated a new apartment in town, and whose teenage son or daughter would get a stipend to study at the university in Sarajevo" (Sudetic 1998, p. 146). While, the wealth of the mines and factories kept men-folk from leaving abroad, it also fuelled enmities between "the area's Muslims and Serbs when decisions had to be made about how it would be divvied up" (Sudetic 1998, p. 139).

Selma Leydesdorff (2015) describes how "Yugoslavia's large debts from the 1970s were due" and that this "led to a national economic crisis" and a recession (p. 30). As money lost its value, and people sought work overseas, especially "the poorer Muslim population of East Bosnia" (Leydesdorff 2015, p. 30). "In the region of Bratunac-Srebrenica, Muslim residents used that money to acquire a large percentage of the land" and this led to anxiety and uncertainty about future and economic social security (Leydesdorff 2015, p. 30). It is in this climate that the "nation's political and administrative structures were also changed rapidly" and "the idea of everyone living together— with their different beliefs, cults and ethnicities—lost political legitimacy" (Leydesdorff 2015, p. 30).

Sudetic (1998) observes that after Yugoslavia's economic collapse and the end of Communism in Yugoslavia, the people in Srebrenica, like most people in the former Yugoslavia, transferred their loyalty to "the new Muslim and Serb nationalist parties in a desperate bid to safeguard their jobs and their futures" (p. 146). This rise of nationalism led to a fracturing of *milieu de mémoire*, the real environments of memory, as everyday spaces once shared by multi ethnic communities—schools, workplaces, marketplaces—were redefined through exclusive ethnic narratives. In Srebrenica, this meant that the collective memory of coexistence gave way to segregated historical identities, paving the way for conflict and eventual violence as competing nationalisms sought to overwrite a pluralist past.

According to the last census conducted before the war, 37,211 people lived in Srebrenica opština or municipality, which consisted of the town and an approximately fifty-square-mile area around it. Seventy-three percent described themselves as Muslims, 25 percent as Serbs, and 2 percent as 'Yugoslavs' or part of no ethnic group" (Rohde 2012, p. xiv).

Sheri Fink (2014) points out that "[a] Serb politician Slobodan Milosević; found that appealing to Serb nationalist sentiment won him support and the leadership of the Serbian Communist Party" (p. 16). Eventually Milosević came to control "half of the votes in the Yugoslav federal government where the leaders of the six republics and two autonomous provinces now shared power" (Fink 2014, p. 16). As other republics held multiparty elections these brought "other ethnicities to office who opposed Serbia's domination" (Fink 2014, p. 16).

Serb nationalist propaganda then flamed ethnic tensions, and in Srebrenica the local party leaders wanted to control Srebrenica's economic assets, and this struggle created further tension between the Muslim and Serb communities. Serb leaders convinced the population that "[w]ith their majority in the local assemblies, the Muslim party leaders could, by law, begin interfering in the management of local enterprises just as the Communist Party bosses had always done" (Sudetic 1998, p. 146). They convinced the Serb population that they would be the first ones to be fired by the Muslim party loyalists and would be left without a job, and since Srebrenica was so isolated with no other jobs around "laid-off men would have no other option than to leave the area and abandon their aged parents in the homes in which many of them had invested their life savings" (Sudetic 1998, p. 146).

The propaganda worked. In his book, *Endgame: The betrayal and fall of Srebrenica, Europe's worst massacre since World II*, David Rohde (2012) shares the perspective of a Serb from Srebrenica who:

> felt that he and his family were discriminated against by the Muslim majority in Srebrenica. His father worked as a miner for twenty-five years but never received a company-owned apartment. Muslims who worked for only five to ten years as miners got them instead. Radić had been unable to find work in town after he graduated from high school, he felt, because he was a Serb (p. 14-15).

This fracturing of identity across ethnic lines meant that the Balkan War was marketed as a religious war by Bosnian Serbs like Radovan Karadžić in order to create nostalgia and longing for a Greater Serbia, but in fact to many of its populace religion played no part in their war-mongering. Fink (2004), for example, suggests that:

> Karadžić, who refers to Bosnian Muslims as the successors of the Ottoman occupiers so resented by the Serbs, is thought by analysts to be using psychiatric theories to create terror in civilian populations and to incite the Bosnian Serb public to violence. Fellow psychiatrists in the United States describe him as a 'malignant narcissist' with dreams of messianic glory (p. 89).

These tensions establish a sense of Nora's concept of fractured memory, as the experience of continuity under Yugoslavia's notion of Brotherhood and Unity was torn apart. The memory of a united Yugoslavia was no longer shared, and instead ethnic memory was created through nationalism, and this division is what paved the way for conflict.

The 1995 genocide during the Bosnian War represents the tearing apart of this *milieude mémoire* and the creation of a new collective identity of the Bosniaks as noted by Assmann that "[c]ultural memory, thus, is clearly connected with the construction of identity: '[o]ne has to remember in order to belong [to a group]" (Assmann 1992, 1999 as cited in Vervaet 2011, p. 3). Within this paradigm the Bosniak identity is constructed through the collective remembrance of trauma, displacement, and loss. The genocide becomes a foundational narrative, shaping a shared memory that both mourns the past and solidifies group cohesion in the present. Cultural memory, then, functions not only as a means of belonging but also as a form of resistance against historical erasure, with commemorations, memorials, and survivor testimonies acting as *lieux de mémoire*—sites where fractured memory is preserved and transmitted across generations. When referring to Bosnian Muslim people in this thesis, I will use the term Bosniak, which refers to an ethnic and cultural designation for a predominantly Muslim population in Bosnia and Herzegovina.

The town of Srebrenica made history on 11 July 1995, when 8,372 men and boys were slain and buried in mass graves, making it the biggest massacre on European soil since World War II as the title of Rohde's book states once again, *Endgame: The betrayal and fall of Srebrenica, Europe's worst massacre since World II* (Rohde 2012). The world is now aware of the genocide, but many people are unaware of the horrors that Srebrenicians endured in the four years preceding it as the Bosniak population lived under siege (Leydesdorff 2011, p. 106).

Before the war, the steep hills that hugged this alpine town were a shelter to the 9,000 residents. During the war, they were the perimeters of what Hasan Hasanovic (2016), a survivor of genocide describes as a "a concentration camp" (p. 34) where over 60,000 refugees (Rhode 2012, p. 45) fought for survival after being ethnically cleansed from nearby areas. Serbs used acts of ethnic cleansing, which is forcibly removing people who shared a common ethnic background from a particular geographical area, in this case any members of the Bosnian Muslim population who lived in Eastern Bosnia.

On the 16 April 1993 the UN was forced to enact a resolution making Srebrenica a safe zone under duress to protect the starving population, however, the UN never provided adequate support or resourcing to make this happen (Rohde 2012, p. 48).

Rohde (2012) details the "Serbs had allowed 30 percent of UN aid convoys to reach their destinations" (p. 72), while Leydesdorff (2005) comments that Doctors without Borders report there were periods when the average daily calories consumed per person amounted to approximately 1,000 in the autumn of 1994 (p. 111). In 1995 those increased, approximately 1,500 calories per day per person were dispensed by the government (Leydesdorff 2005 p. 111). Sells (1996) confirms that "[f]or more than a year, the Muslims in Srebrenica lived in hunger and fear as the Serb army blocked most UN convoys to the besieged enclave, and the UN commanders refused to use their authorised 'necessary means' to break the blockade" (p. 27).

For the next two years, while Srebrenica was designated a safe zone by the UN, the Serbs encircled the enclave from the mountains above, attempting to starve the population into submission by stopping food convoys, determined to take this mineral-rich town for the Serb republic.

This stalemate continued until July 1995, and as peace was being negotiated, with Sudetic (1998) reporting that"United States had a month earlier patched together an uneasy peace between Bosnia's Muslims and Croats" (p. 232), Mladić knew "he needed to hurry" and "relaunch his campaign to drive the Muslims from eastern Bosnia and force Muslim leaders in Sarajevo to capitulate" (Sudetic 1998, p. 231) and so the Serbs made plans to enact their 'final' solution against the Muslim population.

Michael Sells (1996) describes the Serb actions in Banja Luka and the end of a "four year cleansing" during which some "500,000 non-Serbs were killed or expelled" when in October 1995 they introduced the "final phase" of killing of the last "20,000 non-Serbs, mostly Bosnian Muslims" who had "survived over three years atrocities and use as slave labourers by Serb nationalists" as the "Bosnian and Croat armies closed in to within a few miles" of the area (p. 10). Even though this occurred months in late October 1995 after the Srebrenica genocide, it echoes the Srebrenica actions by Serbs and demonstrate they had developed a practiced solution to mass killings.

Rohde (2012) asserts that the "Bosnian Serb leadership had apparently decided to bring the war to a spectacular conclusion that summer" as the "Muslims were only growing stronger with time" (p. 188). Their strategy was "Serb tanks would have sweep through eastern Bosnia and eliminate Srebrenica, Žepa and Goražde" to "finally complete their central goal from the outset of the war" of "creating a 'ethnically pure' strip of Serb-only territory" (Rohde 2012, p. 188). Rohde (2012) continues that:

> Only massive NATO air strikes, could stop them, but with the fall of Srebrenica, the number of cards Mladić held had mushroomed spectacularly. He now had 430 Dutch peacekeepers and 25,000 Muslims he could threaten to kill if NATO planes bombed his troops (p. 188).

On the 6 July 1995, the Serb forces advanced on Srebrenica. Leydesdorff (2015) describes how desperate citizens evacuated the city and trekked the five kilometres to the UN base where a DutchBattalion (Dutchbat) under the command of the United Nations Protection Force (UNPROFOR) were stationed in Potočari, in what was once a battery factory in a former industrial complex (p. 152). They viewed this as their last refuge and so 20,000-30,000 citizens gathered, seeking shelter and protection from 800 Dutch soldiers. On 13 July 1995 the Serbs evacuated all women and young children from the area, and all the men were massacred (Leydesdorff 2015, p. 152).

Dutchbat's mission was to execute United Nations Security Council Resolution 819 in the Bosnian Muslim enclave, which was dubbed a 'safe area' (Rohde 2012, p. 48). The Rules of Engagement stated that the peacekeepers could use force for self-defence only, and that all NATO and UN troops were forbidden from intervening in the fighting because the Clinton administration "feared being drawn into the conflict" (Rohde 2012, p. 48). Rohde (2012) reports that the Dutch were full of resentment as they "were stationed in hell compared with other peacekeepers" who had "all the food and beer they wanted, tennis courts and swimming pools on the main base at Camp Bleso" in Zagreb while the UN didn't even "supply them properly" (p. 106). While the Dutchbat were woefully outnumbered and threatened by the Serb forces and were not supported by the UN in protecting the residents of Srebrenica with airstrikes, there were also reports of soldiers celebrating the fall of the enclave as it meant their tour had ended (Leydesdorff 2015, p. 156).

Roy Gutman (1993a) suggests that the Balkan War of 1992-1995 was "the most vicious conflict seen in Europe or nearly anywhere else since World War II" (p. xvii). While the war raged and atrocities were committed, the Western world prevaricated, however, it was the Srebrenica massacre that led to the unanimous ruling that the massacre of the enclave's male inhabitants constituted genocide, a crime under international law, in 2004 in the case of Prosecutor v. Krstić in the Appeals Chamber of the ICTY (Prosecutor v. Krstić 2004).

As a result, this event is historically significant as it is first genocide conviction in Europe since the Holocaust. It is a globally significant event as it represents the catastrophic failure of the international community to prevent genocide, despite numerous warnings.

Sells (1996) contends that the goal of Serbs "was the eradication of a people and all evidence of that people's culture and existence" (p. 5). And that since "April 1992 the Serb army has targeted for destruction the major libraries, manuscript collections, museums and other cultural institutions in Sarajevo, Mostar, and other besieged cities" (Sells 1996, p. 3. Furthermore, that "[b]etween them, the Croat and Serb nationalists have destroyed an estimated fourteen hundred mosques" (Sells 1996, p. 3). Sells also (1996) argues that "the shelling of these cultural institutions was purposeful" and the "areas around them were left untouched" (p. 2).

Hariz Halilovich (2016) confirms that "The violence behind the destruction was not some spontaneous rampage, but a diligently planned and executed military campaign aimed at erasing any evidence that those who were ethnically cleansed once existed" (Becirevic 2014; Hoare 2008 as cited by Halilovich, p. 82).

In the International Criminal Tribunal for the Former Yugoslavia [ICTY] (*Prosecutor v. Kunarac, Kovac and Vukovic* 2001) "Prosecution witnesses testified that every mosque in Foča was destroyed, one after the other" and that:

> As a consequence of the concerted effect of the attack upon the civilian population of Foča and surrounding municipalities, all traces of Muslim presence in the area were effectively wiped out. Muslim civilians, but for a handful, had been one way or another expelled from the region. According to the 1991 Census, Foča municipality had a pre-war population of about 40,513 inhabitants of whom 52% were Muslim. According to the Prosecutor's evidence, only about ten Muslims remained at the end of the conflict. Witness DR conceded that none of her Muslim friends lived in Foča anymore. In January 1994, Foča was renamed Srbinje by reference to the fact that it is now almost exclusively inhabited by Serbs. The town is now part of Republika Srpska (p. 30).

The example of what occurred in Foča, Banja Luka and Srebrenica demonstrate a clear and deliberate attempt to clear Muslims from desired territories to be able to create a homogenous Serb territory and "to destroy the legacy and memory of Bosnian history through the systematic obliteration of archives and cultural heritage" which has been named "memoricide" (As cited by Lovrenovic 1994, in Halilovich 2016 p. 82). Halilovich explains that many Bosnians have responded to the destruction of key cultural landmarks, such as Vijećnica (the Sarajevo National library), during the Bosnian war which represent their collective identity and cultural memory by incorporating these events "into their own personal memories and narratives" even though they weren't there (Halilovich 2016 , p. 83).

Varvaet (2011) when paraphrasing Enver Kazaz who observed by "creating a history from below, Bosnian war writing counters big history and ;the ideological postulate of grand narratives" (Kazaz 2004 as cited on p. 7). Vervaet (2011) concludes that "literature has the ability to circulate memories of certain historical events" and "turn them into sites of memory" so that they are remembered in the long term" (p. 7). In this way these novels function as a way of commemorating the genocide of Srebrenica and transforming them into sites of memory for Bosnian and non-Bosnian readers.

This is particularly relevant to Srebrenica as there was a deliberate campaign to cleanse the Bosnians from this desired enclave through brutal methods of starvation and massacre, and as a result Srebrenicians lost not only their loved ones and their homes but also their memories, mementos and connections to community. When Leydesdorff (2015) extensively interviewed female survivors about their loss, she found that the trauma of these women saying goodbye to their men-folk who became victims of the massacre was "like a film that was being played repeatedly. The trauma is not part of her life story it has never been integrated" and that this is a "characteristic o f those who have suffered trauma" (p. 147). She explores the psychological process of trauma recovery and how victims need to make sense of traumatic events by integrating them into their life stories, turning them into a part of their past. However, this process is challenging because the trauma often feels disconnected from reality (Leydesdorff 2015, p. 147).

As such the massacre was a deliberate erasure of the cultural and historical memory of Bosniaks by enacting a brutal massacre to ensure that its population would see the town itself as a site of trauma and not return. Adna Karamehić-Oates (2023) reports that:

> Over half of Bosnia's 4.3 million people were driven from their homes as a result of the conflict; of this number, over a million were internally displaced while the rest became refugees. According to estimates by Bosnian authorities, at least 2 million people originating from Bosnia currently live outside the country (p. 7).

In her interviews with women who were living in miserable conditions in a refugee camp Leydesdorff (2015) noted the women's fears "[h]ow can you feel safe in Srebrenica when those in power since the war and the Dayton Accords are the same ones who tried to murder you?" (p. 16-17).

The massacre broke the continuity of the town as a multiethnic society that was united under Yugoslavia and instead transformed it into a site of division and loss, which aligns with Nora's concept of memory becoming torn. The war and genocide severed the natural connection between Srebrenica's pre-war identity and its future, fundamentally altering the way its history is remembered and experienced.

In post-war Bosnia, Srebrenica once a *milieu de mémoire*, has transformed into a *lieux de mémoire* —a symbol of trauma, genocide, and international failure under the Serb Republic (*Republika Srpska*), one of the two entities that makes up the country. This creates a complex and conflicted landscape of memory. The Srebrenica-Potočari

Memorial and Cemetery, where the victims of the genocide are buried is a memorial-cemetery complex in Srebrenica set up to honour the victims of the 1995 Srebrenica massacre. The victims—at least 8,372 of them—were mainly male, mostly Muslim Bosniaks the Memorial Center Srebrenica website reports that "[t]o date, 94 mass gravesites have been exhumed in and around Srebrenica, and 6,900 victims have been positively identified. The search continues, however, for more than 1,700 victims who are still missing" (Memorial Center Srebrenica n.d.).

While the men of Srebrenica were being transported to the killing fields, the women of Srebrenica were transported to the free territory of Tuzla and were living in tents at the airport. After the massacre these women didn't have "an opportunity to read anything about Srebrenica in an entire year and didn't have televisions to watch" (Sudetic 1998, p 342). They were ignorant of reports about the massacre as "Bosnia's Muslim leaders, afraid they might be called to account for the military fiasco that led to the deaths of about eight thousand people, had buried the issue"(Sudetic 1998, p 343-344). In fact, the only information they had about what had happened to their menfolk was "from the visions of fortune-tellers, from *hodža* using secret numbers and tattered books, and from men who survived and found their way across the battlefront. The women passed their information from one to the next" (Sudetic 1998, p 342). Sudetic thus describes the desperation of the women-folk turning to faux religious rituals with a *hodža*, Imam, using numerology and the Quran as a way of divining their future, a ritual labelled as superstition and forbidden under Islam.

One year after the massacre, a memorial service and fundraising event was organised by the Queen Noor of Jordan and Swanee Hunt, the socialite U.S. ambassador to Austria, together with Fatima Huseinovic who was president of Women of Srebrenica, which "yielded a $5 million pledge in U.S. aid, plus $2.5 million from the European Union" (Simons 1996). Amra Begić Fazlić, Deputy Director of the Srebrenica Memorial Center, explained that it was their activism that "led to the establishment of the Memorial Center in 2000" (Arolsen Archives 2022).

During the memorial women saw footage from a tape General Mladic's cameraman had shot of them in the battery factory in Potočari on 12 July 1995, as well as the footage of men surrendering in Kravica. As they watched, "Both sides of the arena erupted in cries of anguish. Women bellowed and covered their eyes with their fingertips and screamed for the tape to stop. 'That's my husband!' a voice in the crowd shouted" (Sudetic 1998, p 343). The women fainted and howled in anguish as they realised that their hope that their menfolk had survived was gone, and that the world had been aware of this long before they were.

Sudetic (1998) reports that he watched this memorial while:

> standing on the basketball floor taking all this down in my notebook, knowing full well that the State Department opposed an exhumation and identification of the remains in the three dozen mass graves around Srebrenica (pp. 344-345).

This marked the first instance of denial of the Srebrenica genocide by both the Bosnian government and the international community. The creation of the memorial at the battery factory in what is now *Republica Srpska* which was the site where the men were taken symbolises a rupture in history—a moment when an entire population was wiped from existence. The memorial itself stands as a deliberate and tangible reminder of the past, with the names of all the victims recorded to ensure their memory is preserved. Each year, newly identified victims are laid to rest, but some will never be found due to the systematic effort by Serb forces to erase evidence of their crimes. In the aftermath of the massacres, bulldozers were used to relocate the bodies to 'secondary' graves, attempting to hide the atrocities from international scrutiny and The Hague (Sudetic, 1998, p. 345). Srebrenica thus functions as a symbol of trauma, genocide, and the international community's failure to prevent it, embodying the concept of *lieux de mémoire*, where memory crystallises and persists despite attempts at erasure.

Furthermore, the memorial in Srebrenica also represents a space where memory is contested by the Serb Republic. The origins of Republika Srpska can be traced back to the disintegration of Yugoslavia in the early 1990s. Sells (1996) notes that on 6-7 April 1992:

> after Bosnians had voted for independence in a referendum, the European Community and the United States recognised Bosnia-Hercegovina as a sovereign state. Meanwhile, Bosnian Serb nationalists had declared their own independent 'Republika Srpska' (Serbian Republic) and set up headquarters in the town of Pale ... with Karadžić as their president and backed by Serbia (p. 9).

Sudetic (1998) notes these were the "political elite of Serbia and Montenegro" a "motley assortment of truck drivers, peasants, herdsmen, 'businessmen', soldiers, teachers, and professionals who had walked out of Bosnia's republican assembly in 1991 and now called themselves the 'parliament of Republika Srpska'" (p. 210).

The Bosnian War, marked by widespread atrocities and ethnic cleansing, saw Republika Srpska playing a significant role in perpetrating violence against Bosniak (Bosnian Muslim) and Croat populations. The political and military leadership of Republika Srpska, led by figures like Radovan Karadžić and General Ratko Mladić, pursued a nationalist agenda that aimed at carving out ethnically homogenous territories, and the ethnic cleanings of Srebrenica was their agenda. This agenda continues: "[i]n Republika Srpska's schools today, genocide denial is still pervasive despite a 2021 law that bans it" (Sabic-El-Rayess 2023, p. 128).

In reaction to this continual denial, in May 2024, United Nations member states voted to declare 11 July as the International Day of Reflection and Commemoration of the 1995 Genocide in Srebrenica (United Nations Security Council 2024). The memorial center commemorates this day through "a week-long program of activities and events which are designed to engage the local, national, and global communities in honouring the victims of the genocide in Srebrenica" as well as "year-round, through research, projects, exhibitions, events, and publications intended to increase public awareness of the genocide" (Memorial Center Srebrenica). In this way the memorial functions to commemorate and educate the public, but also to be a visible symbol that stands against genocide denial by Republika Srpska who now occupy Srebrenica.

This distortion or denial of memory reflects Nora's idea that when memory is no longer naturally sustained, it becomes fragmented and politicised, often dependent on who controls the narrative. In what is now Srebrenica, the administration of Republic Srpska are the ones who control the narrative and are contesting this as a site of genocide, which is in conflict with the testimonies of Bosniak Srebrenician residents and the international community's evidence of Srebrenica as a site of genocide.

The town of Srebrenica itself, now largely inhabited by Serbs, is a shadow of its former self and represents an erasure of the Bosniak-Muslim past. There is no current census data for Srebrenica available however before the war there were 36,600 people in the Srebrenica district "of whom 25,000 were Bosniaks and 8,500 were Serbs" (Vulliamy 2005). In 2005 the population was "10,000, of whom 6,000 are Serbs and 4,000 returnee Muslims" who live in the surrounding villages, "making Srebrenica itself an almost entirely Serbian town" (Vulliamy 2005). At that time, the zinc mine was reopened and contracted to a Russian firm and only employed Serbs, with Bosniak returnees being ineligible, thus reducing employment opportunities and ensuring that Bosniaks wouldn't return to their former city (Vulliamy 2005).

The town represents loss to many of the survivors and descendants of the massacre and so they are unable to return home. In this sense, the physical town no longer serves as a natural environment of memory for its pre-war residents. Instead, it has become a symbol of what has been lost—a physical place that requires active preservation of memory through the commemorations at the memorial, and oral histories shared by the survivors.

The genocide has frozen the town in time, transforming it into a global *lieu demémoire,* a place for remembering not only the atrocity itself but also the broader themes of genocide, war crimes, and the failures of international intervention. The physical remnants of Srebrenica, the cemeteries in the memorial, and the narratives of survivors that the memorial also preserves are crucial in sustaining this memory because the natural, lived memory has been so deeply ruptured.

Furthermore, fictional narratives also contribute to sustaining this memory, which is why it is so significant if the authors are misinformed or wrong. Amra Sabic-El-Rayess(2023) argues that storytelling has a role "in the process of healing, recognition, inclusion and empowerment of Bosniaks deracinated by the Bosnian Genocide" (p. 123). Sabic-El-Rayess (2023) further contends that:

> Being objective in presenting the facts and knowledge is critical but as Christiane Amanpour argues, objectivity cannot be equated to neutrality. This work thus follows that logic because the stories and reflections of the genocide survivors cannot be neutral if they are to be told truthfully and objectively (p. 130).

In this way, fiction has a role in bearing witness to historical trauma, as well as challenging denialist narratives, and when written responsibly, it offers a form of emotional truth that complements factual testimony and contributes to the collective memory of genocide. However, when fiction is shaped by misinformation, erasure, or outsider assumptions, it risks distorting historical realities and further marginalising survivor voices.

The town of Srebrenica before the war was a living, organic *milieu de mémoire*, where memory was naturally embedded in daily life. The genocide shattered this connection, and now, under the Serb Republic, Srebrenica has become a *lieude mémoire*—a deliberately constructed site of memory, fraught with conflicting narratives and the struggle to maintain historical truth against efforts of erasure and denial. As such, the Srebrenica massacre, and the town itself, constitutes a historically significant event and novels written about Srebrenica are historical novels because they serve to memorialise this event for readers, and through this are presenting marginal and dissident accounts of the past.

The Siege Begins: Survival in Srebrenica

The story of Srebrenica is most often remembered for its devastating conclusion—the July 1995 genocide in which more than 8,000 Bosniak men and boys were executed. However, what preceded this atrocity was a prolonged period of systematic deprivation, isolation, and psychological torment endured by the town's residents. From the collapse of infrastructure to starvation, black market corruption, and medical collapse, the people of Srebrenica lived under siege conditions that mirrored medieval suffering. This essay explores the lived experience of survival in Srebrenica, drawing on eyewitness accounts, journalistic testimony, and scholarly research to reveal the brutal reality of life inside the so-called 'safe zone,' and the profound failure of international intervention that allowed this humanitarian catastrophe to unfold.

When war came to Srebrenica, it came painfully and brutally as all of its magnificent geography became a weapon. Rohde (2012) states that:

> At first glance, the enclave's beautiful, but jagged terrain favoured whoever was trying to defend the town. The road from the south ran along the top of a narrow

> ridge. There were sharp, 500-foot- drop-offs on either side. ... The Bosnian Serbs held the peaks ringing the safe area, and the terrain was an artillery man's dream. A moderately skilled gunner could see his potential target directly below. Even if a first shot missed, the second or third could easily be adjusted to hit home (p. 62-63).

The Serbs "had become impatient and decided to take Srebrenica" and on 5 April 1992, they renewed their attack by shelling the town and the hospital. "The water supply was cut off when advancing Serbs captured the water purification plant at Zeleni Jadar, kilometres south of Srebrenica. Although Muslim forces recaptured the site the next day, they could not restore the town's water supply as the Serbs had mined the plant" (Honig and Both 1996, p. 94).

Its isolation favoured the enemy with the only way that its citizens could try to get aid was through ham radio operators who reported "that tens of thousands of displaced Muslims desperately need medical assistance and are in danger of being overrun by Serb forces" (Fink 2003, p. 86). While representatives of the UN High Commissioner for Refugees attempted to negotiate access to Srebrenica and set out several times to reach the town, however they "were forced to turn around when Serb military and angry Serb civilians blocked their convoys" (Fink 2003, p. 86). This led "the head of the UN refugee mission in Belgrade" to conclude "that, for whatever reasons, the Serbs are particularly determined that Srebrenica not receive aid" (Fink 2003, p. 86). By November 1992 Srebrenica and the enclave had not received "any international assistance since the war began, more than seven months ago (Fink 2003, p. 86).

As the world forgot about Srebrenica, its residents were fighting off starvation, eating one or rarely two meals a day and wandering aimlessly around. As the summer days became longer, they spent the days resting, stomach cramps rousing them, and they underwent a physical transformation with their faces losing natural colour, their complexion became bloodless and almost featureless, with grey wrinkled skin and dark circles around their tired gaze (Suljagic 2005, p. 32-33).

Forced by desperation, residents began saying that they "were off to gather food" in that first long year of war. Emir Suljagic (2005) describes these danger-filled journeys in his first-person account of surviving the siege, *Postcards from the Grave*, with residents setting off on long journeys from Srebrenica to the villages, walking on forest paths in the dark, searching for "un-plundered farms and cellars for bits of food" (p. 39-40).

The road they walked on literally went through Serb bunkers with whole families travelling, hoping they would survive and bring enough food back to spare them another trip. Serb forces let them pass to gather food and then trapped them in an ambush on the way back when they were exhausted from carrying heavy loads and were close enough for the Bosnian forces to hear the firing, but too far to help (Suljagic 2005, p. 39-40).

Sudetic (1998) reports that desperate refugees slipped through Serb lines to steal food from Serbs and that "[o]ne group had crawled into a wheat field just outside Bratunac in late summer. Quietly, these refugees used paper scissors to snip off all the spikes of grain, and the next morning the farmer awoke to find amber waves of beheaded stalks" (p. 157).

Corruption, Privilege, and the Black Market Economy

As the ring around Srebrenica tightened, internally it seethed with corruption running rife and crimes, including murder, soared. The town was divided between the haves and have-nots and while the president of the Municipal council showed off cardboard packs of Marlboro bought from Canadian and Dutch soldiers, Suljagic and his friends were making cigarettes out of bad paper and bitter home-grown tobacco that pinched the throat and burned into black ashes. Some municipal-council officials drove in cars while people walked dozens of kilometres wearing bad shoes (Suljagic 2005, p. 30-31).

By July 1992, black market prices soared with trades being arranged and one box of matches was equal to 10 kg potatoes, or ten eggs, or a kilo of cheese. As all the white flour was used up, residents turned to wholemeal, then maize flour, then oats which were impossible to grind. The flour was bitter and made throats sore, then as this too was used up, then they turned to stalks and hazel bushes that were ground up in water mills (Suljagic 2005, p. 34).

Hasan Nuhanovic (2019) in his memoir *The Last Refuge: A True Story of War, Survival and Life Under Siege in Srebrenica* describes the marketplace as "a scene of absolute confusion—dirt, shards of glass, horse dung, large chunks of plaster that had fallen off buildings, and people in ragged clothes and shoes. Worn-out shoes were maintained by wrapping pieces of rug or sheep or cow skin around them which were then secured with string" (p. 171).

This was "the liveliest part of town" "where all trade was done" and the reason "why so many people ended up being killed there" (Nuhanovic 2019, p. 171). The market place was where people came to get news and information such as "where to get the cheapest corn, in which burned-out Muslim village could you still find food, where the Chetniks were positioned, what had been on the news the night before, whether NATO was going to intervene or when the war was going to be over" (Nuhanovic 2019, p. 171). Chetniks were Serb paramilitary groups.

The residents "from the undamaged mountain villages gathered to sell corn, potatoes and eggs" and a single egg sold for ten Deutschmarks or a kilogram of shucked corn; "almost all the tobacco sellers were armed, as tobacco had reached the price of three thousand marks a kilogram" (Nuhanovic 2019, p. 171). Everyone preferred German currency to US dollars and "new banknotes were not entering Srebrenica, it was always the same ones being circulated, so even they were worn out and torn" (Nuhanovic 2019, p. 171).

By the end of winter 1992 "cigarettes became the solid currencies and life revolved around them—you could pay and get paid" (Suljagic 2005, p. 36-37). A pack of cigarettes became the equivalent of 150 or 200 Deutschmarks. As money lost meaning residents began sewing plant pots during the summer on their balconies, they picked leaves every morning from the bottom upwards, dried them on a cooking stove, crumbled the dry but still green leaves onto pages of a newspaper.

Some smoked quinces or apple-tree leaves, coltsfoot leaves, leaves of nettles, plantains or any plant at all. When the UN Forces arrived, cigarettes got cheaper. In the first week, they were 50 marks a packet, then down to 10-15 marks depending on the brand. Canadians, then Dutch bought cigarettes at their canteen for 2 marks, then sold them to black marketeers for 5, who sold them at two or three times worth that to those who could afford it (Suljagic 2005, p. 36-37). Others started cutting up the Red Cross stationery and tearing out pages from old books to roll cigarettes filled with pumpkin leaves (Sudetic 1998, p. 219).

As desperation forced residents to contemplate any food, including grinding up actual cobs to eat "constipation became a common affliction and some people even died from it" (Nuhanovic 2019, p. 144). The only treatment available was "inserting a rubber hose into a patient's anus and letting water flow into their bowels to help loosen their stool. From what I'd heard those beyond help died in terrible agony" (Nuhanovic 2019, p. 144).

Destruction of war

War brought with it the harbingers of destruction, aeroplane bombs that rained down death and terror. In the first attack that lasted only five to ten minutes, a mother and son were standing a couple of metres from the concrete school playground when the bombs hit. They had to scrape what remained of them with shovels. Three weeks later, there was another attack. As the fog dispersed a jet plane flew over the town at high speed, breaking the sound barrier, dropping bombs on their next pass, disappearing as quickly as they appeared, leaving behind demolished buildings, human bodies shredded by bombs, big craters. Some planes announced themselves by the buzz of engines, disparagingly called 'mosquitoes' because they were sporting or farming planes which Serbs had equipped with machine guns and stuffed with bombs (Suljagic 2005, p. 42-45).

In the monotony of war young people hungered for recreation, and Suljagic (2005) describes desperate visits to the school library by getting in through broken windows and stepping over shards of glass, then creeping through school corridors and classroom, while listening to the sky "we stopped breathing at every rustle and were ever quicker to leave the building. We knew that no good for us came from the sky" (p. 46). The school library fell victim to a 'boiler' which was what the improvised bombs were dubbed. These dropped from great height and exploded on the slopes near town, and one of these literally ripped the school building in two, leaving its smaller part still standing, separated by a gap as large as a hand (Suljagic 2005, p. 46).

As the town became isolated the only way to communicate was to make a phone call by lining up in front of the "small yellow building in the centre of the town" which had a huge aerial on the roof that connected the "rickety army-green radio set" that was run by a radio operator who would only allow five minute phone calls to desperate citizens (Suljagic 2005, p. 47).

Salt Ban and its Effects

In the winter of 1992, salt became a rare commodity as Serbs prevented salt from entering the enclave, and it sold on the black market for 50 Deutschmarks, making the corrupt officials rich (Suljagic 2005, p. 50). Sudetic (1998) reported that "the fact that folks in the Drina valley had for generations been nicknamed the people of Srebrenica "goiters" did not go unnoticed by Serb military commanders (p. 243). He reported a leaked copy of a Yugoslav army document pertaining to the lack of salt in the Srebrenica area which were the findings of the military scientific research team that tested and analysed the drinking water and natural springs in the Drina valley with the results showing that the water has a low iodine content. "Thus, the deprivation of salt from the diet will lead to a number of malfunctions in the so-called endocrine organs and in the psychological area will lead persons to experience confusion, instability and aggressiveness—an inclination toward anarchy and panic; and a susceptibility to psychological manipulation" (Sudetic 1998, p. 243).

The practical effects of this deprivation were that Srebrenica's Muslims were prevented from "preserving their meat, cabbage, peppers and other vegetables for the winter, and without food reserves they were susceptible to hunger and boredom and pressure to leave the enclave" (Sudetic 1998, p. 243). The only salt available was slabs of rock salt that was used on the roads in winter, which did not contain iodine (Nuhanovic 2019, p. 146).

The only lifeline Srebrenicians had were the convoys that arrived a few times a week and provided the necessities of life with "flour, less often salt, juice powder, Ikar brand cans, clothes, footwear, cleaning, products, soap" (Suljagic 2005, p. 66-68). Suljagic (2005) describes that the day after a convoy humanitarian aid would end up on market-stalls that were full of shiny packets of orange-juice powder or big tins of oils. Only once did the police carry out a raid and arrest the people trading in humanitarian aid (p. 66-68).

The trucks were used as evacuation trucks with desperate civilians cramming on "truck trailers, piled on top of each other, wearing all the clothes they possessed, with a couple of bags to fit their whole lives, set of an on journey of several hundred kilometres" with children suffocating along the way (Suljagic 2005, p. 69-73).

Eventually, these evacuations were stopped by the Bosnian government who worried that "[i]f the evacuations from Srebrenica continued at this rate, there would soon be no substantial civilian population left" (Honig and Both 1996, p. 92).

War Hospitals in Medieval Conditions

As the city descended into war-time conditions, the war hospital operated in medieval conditions. Antibiotics are brought into the hospital by not-for-profit organisations but are not available to patients. Instead, the life-saving penicillin is sold on the black market with desperate family members finding where to buy it, or if they are without funds, they consider killing to get the drugs they need (Fink 2003, p. 116). Sheri Fink in her book *War Hospital* describes a doctor

Nedret examining a patient with a groin injury who was stuck in the woods outside of Srebrenica and has developed a dangerous infection. The doctor has no antibiotics to prescribe. The next day the patient "shows him a small bottle containing an injection of four million international units of penicillin. The vial looks suspiciously like the penicillin Nedret brought with him when he entered Srebrenica last summer. He demands to know where it came from, but the patient refuses to tell him" (Fink 2003, p. 116).

A doctor, Thierry, who uses his vacation time to volunteer with the Médecins Sans Frontières (Doctors without Borders) is "mortified by the situation" in Srebrenica hospital and "simply cannot believe his eyes" (Fink 2003, p. 151). "A seasoned urologist with a steady stomach for foul smells, he is nonetheless overwhelmed by the stench of Srebrenica Hospital. Every time he cracks open the hospital door, it takes him several minutes to catch his breath and habituate to the doors of death and gangrene before he can force himself to walk inside" (Fink 2003, p. 151). He finds himself wondering how is this possible in Europe, "at the end of the twentieth century" (Fink 2003, p. 151).

The hospital is filled beyond capacity with additional buildings being used to take overfill. Morale is non-existent from "the cumulative effects of a year of war, loss of hope or pure physical degradation from exhaustion, extreme stress, and lack of food" in the "apathetic and impassive staff members" who ask him "[w]hy should we work?" because "[w]e will all die anyway" (Fink 2003, p. 151). Their approach "to performing medicine is hands-off at best" with no "regular schedule of morning and evening rounds" and "the hierarchy of experience and responsibility, has, to Thierry's eyes, drifted into chaos and disorganisation" (Fink 2003, p. 152).

The lice infested hospital stirs during the night when they "begin to stir and bite, invisible creeps-crawlies scuttling their way over the skin of patients and doctors" (Fink 2003, p. 71-72). Within the hospital the only source of light which are pieces of "oil-soaked cotton smoulder in coffee cups or medicine bottles exhaling a smoky light" where the "doctors feel rather than see their way around the cavernous hospital" (Fink 2003, p. 71-72). It is "too dark to remove the bodies of patients who die" (Fink 2003, p. 71-72) and so they will remain there until the morning, sharing space with the living.

When a German photographer "whose bumbling ways and repeated injuries" led to the nickname "grenade magnet" woke up from a ketamine anaesthesia after surgery he described "a beautiful dream" where "he was flying and the earth below looked like a beautiful ball" (Fink 2003, p. 164). He was asked whether "Bosnia was on that earth" (Fink 2003, p. 164) demonstrating the hopelessness and despair of its residents who felt they were wiped off the face of the earth.

Hydrogen peroxide which is "used in the production of rockets and torpedoes, paper, chemicals and car batteries" is found in an "abandoned battery factory up the road" and used in the operating room as a steriliser to help prevent "one out of three amputation patients dying from infection or blood loss" and is dubbed "Bosnia's greatest war hero" by a doctor at the hospital (Fink 2003, p. 5).

Even though morale within the "ad hoc troops defending the territory around Srebrenica" is lifted because they have qualified surgeons in the "Srebrenica war hospital" so that "[a]mputations take place in the hospital room rather than on the kitchen tables or living room floors of village houses where they did the first three months of war" (Fink 2003, p. 9). However, "medical care is still in the Middle Ages. A head, chest, or stomach wound means near-certain death. As more soldiers realise this and lose the will to fight, their commanders believe there is more of a chance that Serb forces will succeed in expelling the Muslims from their land" (Fink 2003, p. 9).

A wounded soldier is carried by his comrades six miles from a battlefield when he was hit with a large bullet from an anti-aircraft gun that has nearly severed his lower arm. The doctor has to amputate "but will try to save some of the limb below the shoulder" (Fink 2003, p. 72).

Fink (2003) describes the amputation that takes place without electricity or anaesthetic "[i]n the operating room, assistants scurry around the doctors, casting eerie shadows" created by "a single light bulb" that "wavers and flickers, powered by a homemade hydroelectric contraption built on the stream that runs through town" (p. 72). The "medical workers hook the patient to an infusion tube the surgeon brought with him and clean his skin with hydrogen peroxide" however there is no general aesthetic and so "they inject a couple of ampoules of local numbing medicine but this has little effect on the patient's pain" the doctor "guesses the medicine sat in the sun too long" (Fink 2003, p. 72).

The arm amputation begins with "the patient wincing in pain" every time the doctor cuts, and the patient shows great fortitude in moaning, but remaining still with no nurses needing to restrain him (Fink 2003, p. 72).

> A few times he asks, "Could you please stop for a moment? I really feel bad" (Fink 2003, p. 72). The doctor saves the worst part for the end, the isolating of the nerves and when he touches one, "the patient jumps as if jolted by an electric shock. A nurse and technician have to hold him down now. The doctors talk to him constantly as they work, "Hold on..." they tell him. The man barely moves as they close his skin with sutures. Normally contaminated war wounds

are left open to drain to avoid infection, and they are closed several days later, Nedret makes the unorthodox choice to close the wound with sutures now and spare the patient another painful procedure" (Fink 2003, p. 72).

Winter in the enclave

When winter came, survival became even more base and primitive. Historically, temperatures in Bosnia during the winter months (November to February) range from -6.0°C to 6.2°C. Fire was a necessity to survival and as desperate residents used up any firewood they had, they then turned to using whatever they could in the house to survive, including burning books, floor parquetry, as well as partitioning off rooms with blankets to preserve much needed heating (Baksic 1995, p. 7). Residents "went to bed fully dressed wearing our woollen sweaters, socks, everything we'd had on during that day" (Nuhanovic 2019, p. 194).

Eventually there was the need to cut wood and so in the early morning, before the fog above the narrow valley dispersed, hundreds would climb hills dressed in dirty rags, stinking of dried sweat, carrying an axe and a rope. Sometimes people would clamber on hands to the top of the cliffs and reach a small, bleak plain. To save energy they would cut the first tree, tie a rope, drag it several hundred metres, until "with great pleasure they would push it off the cliff and then following goat tracks they would descend slowly in pursuit of it. When they reached the bottom, they'd drag it home through town (Suljagic 2005, p. 42).

As winter came, Srebrenica descended into a medieval town with the snow covering the ruins, with the thousands of displaced refugees resembling a "Dickensian" scene:

> Smoke stains accent the windowless, grey-faced buildings like eye shadow over empty eye sockets. Scavenged cars are banked on the snowy side streets. Mangy dogs weave back and forth between piles of trash. The streets are littered with empty brown plastic meal packages from the airdrops whose contents have been devoured on the spot. Groups of people camp out in the freezing cold. Last night saw them dotting the road, setting quick-burning plastic crates afire for some semblance of warmth. This morning, faces and palms stained black, they wander aimlessly while new arrivals-tarrying bundles pulling rough wooden sledges leading horses, and pushing wheelbarrows and sleigh-bottomed carts-search for a place to stop and live (Fink 2003, p 133).

"Women wear layers of sweaters in lieu of coats, scarves around their heads and mud-covered baggy *dimije* on their legs. They walk in rubber boots bent under immense bundles holding babies in their arms. Children, some wearing socks but no shoes, carry their own, smaller bundles" (Fink 2003, p 133).

As food deprivations hit "malnourished children die from common colds," and "an orphaned baby perishes of acute starvation" (Fink 2003, p 114). The hospital patient and staff didn't have enough food "despite the donations of generous villagers with land" and non-injured come to the hospital "desperate for food" (Fink 2003, p 114).

Air-Dropped Hope: Chaos and Competition for Aid

In September 1993, Sarajevo Bosnia's Muslim-led government boycotted humanitarian aid supplies to Sarajevo until U.N. relief convoys provided emergency food and medical supplies to starving Muslims trapped by Serb forces in eastern Bosnia. It took nine days for the aid boycott to succeed and the "White House announced it would parachute food and medicine into Srebrenica and other Eastern Bosnian enclaves despite the UN official's objections" who argued for neutrality (Sudetic 1998, p. 174).

Initially, Naser Orić, a Bosnian former officer who commanded the Army of the Republic of Bosnia and Herzegovina (ARBiH) forces in Srebrenica, attempted to "organise equitable distribution of food" by announcing that each person would receive food for one meal a day (Sudetic 1998, p. 177). He banned civilians from the drop zones and had work brigades "recover sacks of wheat flour from the parachuted pallets and transport them to the department store for distribution" (Sudetic 1998, p. 177).

However, "[s]oldiers, officers, civilian members of work brigades pilfered food for their own families, hiding sacks of flour in snow drifts and carrying them by through the woods to their homes" and so "by the time food arrived at the department store there was never enough" (Sudetic 1998, p. 178). Civil unrest erupted with fist fights, threats being exchanged and "weapons brandished" (Sudetic 1998, p. 178).

Thierry Pontus, a doctor with MSF, detailed his experiences of a food drop and that he:

> quickly realised that the greatest danger came from competition for the packages. Groups had formed, and an unarmed individual had almost no chance of obtaining a package or, if he acquired one, holding on to it. The local government was powerless to stop such violence within the enclave. There was also the danger of being hit by a falling pallet of packages, in the dark, one could neither see nor hear the pallets as they were dropped. Darkness was mandatory; a flashlight made one a sniper's target (Leydesdorff 2011, p. 123-124).

After ten days, it was announced that it was everyone for himself and so "[m]ountain sides now flickered with the flames of a legion of torches each night as desperate people streamed through the drifts to the drop areas" (Sudetic 1998, p. 178). Fink describes "an unreal sight-long, black snakes wriggling slowly across the snowy white mountainside" (Fink 2003, p. 130) who are "lines of hungry exhausted Srebrenica residents who struggle up the mountain desperate for manna-like provisions falling from the sky" (Fink 2003, p. 131).

The new refugees who were from Konjević Polje, many of whom were widows with children, didn't have the energy to fight for food. Word got back to Rhein-Main air base that the "weakest were still going hungry" and "[m]en were killing one another in forests to get flour" and that "falling pallets, as big as two refrigerators smashed into the ground at eighty-give miles an hour" crushing those who risked "waiting inside the landing zones to get food first" (Sudetic 1998, p. 178). The Americans responded by doubling the number of air-supply missions, flying at low altitude and dropping tens of thousands of individual meals in brown plastic wrappers (Sudetic 1998, p. 178).

General Morillon's Visit: False Promises and Public Desperation

As ham operators desperately relay news of starving residents, General Morillon, commander of the United Nations Forces in Bosnia (1992-1993), sets out "to visit the besieged eastern Bosnian pockets of Ćerska and Konjević Polje. On his return, he holds a press conference surprising the journalists with his impression that conditions are not as serious as ham radio reports have suggested" and the Serbs agree to an evacuation after his statement (Fink 2003, p. 122).

"Over the next days the general's blasé comments provoke public outcry from U.N refugee officials" (Fink 2003, p. 122). When one of the General's own travelling party, a physician, makes his own way to Srebrenica and reports that "the medical care as more primitive than anything he has seen in war-ravaged Afghanistan or Liberia. Up to thirty people a day are dying of disease exacerbated by malnutrition. Roughly 200 people require immediate evacuation and 2,000 sick and injured" (Fink 2003, p. 122). These reports are circulated to the media and "[n]ow it is General Morillon's assessment that looks foolish and naive" (Fink 2003, p. 122). Morillon is now determined to visit Srebrenica for himself and claims he "will go to Srebrenica, if necessary, even by foot" (Fink 2003, p. 123).

Rohde (2012) reports that "Morillon had no permission to go to Srebrenica from his superiors, who feared making UN promises that peacekeepers couldn't keep. ...Even after all the reports they were genuinely stunned by the misery they found." (p. 45-46).

Fink (2003) reports that "[u]pon arrival, Morillon is offered what 'passes for bread' in Srebrenica – the hard, terrible-tasting loaves made from corncobs, hazelnut tree catkins, beech tree buds, or dried apple and pear pulp milled on water-powered grinding stones" (p. 129).

While Suljagic (2005) continues that as he eats a "a slice of hazel-bush bread, he says a little embarrassed 'healthy food, good for the digestion'" (p. 34).

Morillon attempts to leave to negotiate a ceasefire, leaving behind "handful of UN military observers and peacekeepers who accompanied him" (Honig and Both, 1996, p. 86) however, "[d]uring Morillon's presence in Srebrenica the Serbs had not fired single shell on the town itself. With the UN general in their midst, the people of Srebrenica had begun to feel more secure. They feared that if he left, the shelling would start again, as had happened in Konjević Polje" (Honig and Both, 1996, p. 86).

The UN commander tried to leave but his car was "was encircled by women and children" a form of protest secretly "ordered by Naser Orić and the town's leaders to prevent Morillon from leaving but to do it in a 'civilised way'" (Rohde 2012, p. 45-46).

Sudetic (1998) reports that Morillon ordered a media release to the press "[f]ully conscious that a major tragedy was about to take place in Srebrenica, I deliberately came here. And I have now decided to stay here in Srebrenica in order to calm the population's anguish in order to try to save them" (p. 181-182).

And so the next morning, on the 12 March 1993, he walked to the balcony of the post office and:

> made his now famous declaration from the post office window—'You are now under the protection of the United Nations…I will never abandon you'—his aides burst out laughing. They knew Morillon did not have permission to make the desperate promise and he had no way to keep it (Rohde 2012, p. 45).

The Schoolyard Massacre: Betrayal in the 'Safe Zone'

On the 12 April 1993, as the Security Council negotiate and vote "U.N- Resolution 816, authorising NATO to shoot down unauthorised aircraft over Bosnia," the residents of Srebrenica embrace a beautiful spring day, enjoying the mild temperature and the blooming of foliage on the surrounding mountains.

Fink (2003) sets the scene and describes:

> Srebrenica residents, the majority of whom have precious little with which to occupy their days, spill out of their cramped quarters and take to the streets. Refugee children from the schoolhouse run to play in the open air, their mothers strolling outside to watch them. Dozens crowd the amphitheatre-like steps that wrap around the schoolyard to watch soccer matches played with balls air-dropped at the suggestion of a UNHCR official. In a far corner of the stands a—knot of young fans surrounds three teens who strum folk songs on a guitar-like shargija (Fink 2003, p. 167).

It is on this peaceful scene that "the first Serb mortar round detonated in the Srebrenica schoolyard where the boys were playing soccer" (Sudetic 1998, p. 202). Sudetic (1998) describes the chaotic scene as:

> A plume of grey smoke and dust vaulted skyward and bits of gravel pelted the ground. Shouts of frenzy

> blasted through the whistling scream that filled the ears of everyone caught by the thunderclap. Shrapnel had torn off legs and arms. Teeth had been ripped from mouths. Severed torsos squirted blood and oozed intestines. Hysterical children screamed and trembled. Parents inside the school rushed outside to the playground to look for their kids. A second shell hit. Flying shreds of flesh splattered onto the white wall of the school and got caught on the playground fence and on nearby trees and poles (p. 202).

Carnage follows with Muslim men loading "bodies and body parts into oxcarts and wheelbarrows to carry them to the hospital" (Sudetic 1998, p. 202). While Fink states that "[s]tories will turn to legend: that one shargija player survived beneath the bodies of his two friends—that blood ran like a river down the street from the schoolhouse to the hospital—that Canadian soldiers patrolling the town in an APC when the shelling began couldn't make it back to their headquarters in the post office because the roads were blocked by bodies. A U.N. refugee official will describe seeing body parts caught in the schoolyard fence" (Fink 2003, p. 168)

What was an even greater betrayal was that the response by UN officials that Muslims had provoked it, with Sudetic (1998) stating that "UN officials in Sarajevo and Zagreb had developed a knack for telling journalists and their superiors—*sotto* voice, of course—that they believed Muslim soldiers provoked the particularly bloody Serb attacks on Muslim civilians. This habit helped mute the calls for serious action that such horrors inevitably elicited" (p. 203).

They told journalists a "story that one of Orić's two tanks had fired its cannon at the Serbs and that the Serbs had shot into the schoolyard only in retaliation" and even though this story was retracted, the damage was done (Sudetic 1998, p. 203). The death and carnage was once again laid at the foot of the victims themselves, a necessary lie for the UN to hide that "progress" that they had reported was not a lie, to counter the fact that "an intense artillery attack on April 12, left fifty-six people dead in Srebrenica. Fourteen children were found dead in the town's schoolyard" (Rohde 2012, p. 47).

To the residents of Srebrenica, the playground massacre would always remain an echo of the horror and betrayal they were constantly subjected to under siege. Years afterward, residents who walked by school ground late at night would report of hearing calls for help and screams for the children who were killed on this day (Sudetic 1998, p. 224).

The Safe Zone Illusion: Coping, Creating, and Enduring

And that's how Srebrenica found itself declared a safe zone that was purportedly protected by the UN, and yet to the residents Morillon's announcement he is "like a trumpeter heralding the arrival of hope" and residents believe they have been saved (Fink 2003, p. 146). Now they turned their attention to surviving under siege and living through the monotony of a war zone.

Suljagic (2005) reports that the lack of electricity was one of "the first problem to be solved, even before UN troops arrived in the town" when "a small, improvised power plant appeared on Crvena Rijeka [the red river], which flows through the town" (p. 129). These power plants were made simply with "a mill wheel, an electric engine and a simple wire, several hundred metres connecting it to the house of its owner" and soon "[e]very village stream was used, and the entire enclave was illuminated again" (Suljagic 2005, p. 129). While the voltage was inconsistent and lights flickered on and off "it was still better than oily cloths that stank and offered only a weak light" (Suljagic 2005, p. 129).

Soon these power plants became more than a necessity but were instead status symbols with those who had more power getting "a proper, regular water intake and big engines, which meant that they could even watch TV and that the light bulbs in their flats did not flicker" however reception was "poor because of the town's geographic position" (Suljagic 2005, p. 129). The town became a spider web of interlaced wires that were "hanging from every lamp post and every building" so that walking became "dangerous, especially when it was raining, snowing or the wind was blowing, because sparking bits of wire would fall off" and there were many unfortunate owners who ended "up in hospital with broken limbs because he had fallen off a tree or a lamp post" trying to fix the connection (Suljagic 2005, p. 129).

Others built a "dam across a creek below the house and rigged up a waterwheel a generator and cables that powered their refrigerator water heater, and television" and even had "running water from the spring" and so could take hot showers (Sudetic 1998, p. 243).

Suljagic (2005) recreates the reality of young people growing up in a war zone and describes his attempts to "cheat hunger by frantically reading or sleeping" and "[s]eeking comfort in acrid home-made rakija that burnt the stomach and destroyed the brain" (p. 28-29). Cigarettes were a way of staving of hunger and seeking recreation and so they "[c]ount the drags that each of them took and argued about the roach" as they grow up "in torn jumpers, stolen shoes, trousers acquired from the plunder of a village not yet burnt down" feeling like they are living on borrowed time as their teeth rot from their war-diet marked by malnutrition (Suljagic 2005, p. 28-29).

The residents seek an escape from the "complete darkness and a raging war" beyond their walls and so a disco opens in the town by one of the families that "ruled the town" (Suljagic 2005, p. 130). The disco does not use a power plant and instead it is powered by "a generator unit that was inaudible inside buildings until late at night" (Suljagic 2005, p. 130). Entry costs "two cigarettes" and a drink of "either humanitarian aid juice, diluted from powder, or plum brandy" cost five marks and everyone attends including "local thugs, officers from the divisional command and often the commander himself" (Suljagic 2005, p. 130).

Residents use the power plants to open cinemas in their living rooms sometimes dividing them "in two, with one or two TVs connected to a VCR" and playing "pre-war stock of Srebrenica's video stores, and the price of entrance was two cigarettes or two tobacco leaves" (Suljagic 2005, p. 130). Residents queued to enter these cinemas "acting as if it were nothing out of the ordinary" sitting on the "the room lit up by the milky white light from the screen, as couples held hands or kissed" imagining that their "cinema could have been anywhere in the world" (Suljagic 2005, p. 130).

Other families used "a wooden wheel about three feet in diameter that was connected by a belt to a pulley and a generator" (Sudetic 1998, p. 236). Members of the family "took turns spinning the wheel by hand to power the VCR and the television set" and "if someone wandered in with no cigarettes he could spin the wheel and thereby earn the right to watch the spaghetti westerns, the kung fu movies with Bruce Lee and Jean-Claude van Damme and old Yugoslav slapstick" (Sudetic 1998, p. 236). From time to time, horse races were organised in Potočari and a "brothel and a handful of cafes threw open their doors" (Sudetic 1998, p. 236).

Nuhanovic (2019) relates how a neighbour of his created a spinning wheel that was connected to "a small battery which, in turn, was hooked up to a cassette player that had a radio built into it. To my great surprise, as the wheel was turned, BiH Radio came out of the speakers" (p. 152). Residents took turns spinning the wheel to listen to the news and find out when they would be saved.

Three young men start a newspaper "Glas Srebrenica [Voice of Srebrenica]" which comes out irregularly and is printed on ordinary A4 paper that is donated by the municipal authorities with text painstakingly typed on the back of forms filled out before (Suljagic 2005, p. 136). Only twenty copies are typed out individually on a typewriter, and only one copy "had a front page in colour, generally drawn with coloured pencils" (Suljagic 2005, p. 136). This newspaper did not feature news, that was what the radio was for, instead "[l]ocal journalists published their first texts and poems, incomprehensible and hard to read" from "grammatical and spelling mistakes and big words such as ·'geopolitical', 'strategic' and 'global', which were used at random, mostly in order to point out how educated and eloquent the author was" (Suljagic 2005, p. 136).

The only way of connecting with the world was through the Red Cross letters, which was a single sheet with "twenty-three dotted lines for a message to be innocuous enough to pass a military censor" (Sudetic 1998, p. 218). Each letter was censored in the local Red Cross office with "with entire paragraphs so thoroughly crossed out with a black marker pen that nothing beneath was legible" (Suljagic 2005, p. 123). It seems the dictionary of forbidden words were ones that "that in fact reflected the essence of our lives: army, killed, perished, Chetniks, executed, slaughtered, captured, hunger, black market, crimes, prostitution, despair ..." (Suljagic 2005, p. 123). To Suljagic (2005) it seems as if "our truth was not a truth for the outside world" (p. 123).

However, not everyone is lucky. There are "hundreds of displaced persons" living in the schoolhouse "packed fifty to sixty to a classroom, sleeping on pushed-together desks under the gaze of the old leader Tito whose framed photographs still adorn the high walls above green chalkboards" (Fink 2003, p. 166). All of these displaced have "itchy rash of skin infested with scabies and about half look anaemic" from the horrific conditions with no showers or baths available and stopped up toilets so that "people defecate in the open" (Fink 2003, p. 166). Diarrhoea runs rampant when "Chetnik soldiers capture Srebrenica's water treatment plant and cut off the merger supply of running water" (Fink 2003, p. 166). "A recently arrived MSP general practitioner takes advantage of the quiet to try to improve the situation in the Srebrenica schoolhouse" by installing a water bladder, organising cleaning of the schoolrooms, and treating "patients with the now-ample supply of drugs" (Fink 2003, p. 166).

And this is how the residents of Srebrenica survived for the next two years, until the fall of Srebrenica, and the massacre that stained its land red, and entered its name in the history books.

The siege of Srebrenica was not only a humanitarian crisis but a profound indictment of international failure. While the town was declared a UN-protected "safe zone," its people were left to starve, suffer, and eventually perish under the gaze of a world that looked away. And yet, amid the devastation, the resilience of Srebrenica's residents stands as a testament to human endurance—they built power plants from river wheels, held cinemas in basements, and shared cigarettes as currency in a collapsed economy. Their will to survive, to love, and to create meaning in the darkest of circumstances demands that we remember Srebrenica not only as a site of genocide, but as a place where a community fought to live. To truly honour their suffering, we must embed their stories in our collective memory and ensure that "never again" is more than an empty refrain.

The Urban / Rural Divide in Yugoslavia

Early in my marriage to my husband I had a conversation with someone who was not Bosnian about the Balkan War. "The Serbs and Bosnians always hated each other" I said, speaking from my limited experience as a former resident having lived in Yugoslavia as a child from 1985 to 1989. "No, they didn't" my Sarajevo-born husband interjected. "Muslims and Serbs worked together and inter-married all the time."

This was the first time that I realised that there were differences in the experiences of those who were from urban area versus those in the rural area. My grandparents came from a small town called Bosanska Gradiška, and the memories of WWII, and the divisions left there were still fresh in their memory, while my husband was from cosmopolitan Sarajevo, a city known for its ethnic mix and cultural tolerance. However, when we look at Srebrenica and the experience of its residence during the siege, this urban and rural division had a key influence in the day-to-day lives of residents in Srebrenica. But first, to understand Srebrenica, we need to set the scene and review the carnage of WWII.

When I lived in Bosnia my grandfather told me stories of being a soldier in WWII. He spoke of Ustashe and Chetniks. About slaughters on the banks of the river Sava that ran through the town of Bosanksa Gradiška and the river running red with blood, but I didn't understand who was who or why they were fighting.

Croatia, Serbia and Bosnia were each initially independent kingdoms. In medieval times came the Ottoman Empire invasion, which absorbed Bosnia and Serbia, while Croatia avoided conquest by electing the King of the Austrian-Hungarian Empire to rule as they had already been united with Hungary for centuries.

Post WWI and in the interwar period before WWII, these countries formed the Kingdom of Yugoslavia, ruled by a Serbian monarch. Yugoslavia literally translates to South Slavs (Jug-South, Slav-people of Slavic ancestry).

During WWII, there were various factions with their own loyalties and agendas. There were the Croatian fascists, Ustasha. The Chetniks who were a somewhat loose alliance of groups of Serb nationalists and royalists who typically sought the establishment of a Greater Serbia cleansed of non-Serbs. And the Partisans, a Communist resistance group, led by Tito.

Joe Sacco (2018) in his graphic novel *Safe Area Goražde* reports that:

> During WWII more than a million Yugoslavs died in the war, mostly at the hands of other Yugoslavs. When the Axis powers occupied and dismembered the Kingdom of Yugoslavia in 1941, they installed the Croatian fascists, the Ustasha, in their own state, which was expanded to include Bosnia. The fury with which the Ustasha carried out their genocidal program of whole state slaughter, forced religious con-

> version, and expulsion of the Serb population left even the Nazis aghast (p. 18).

The Ustashe were responsible for creating extermination camps and from August 1941 to April 1945 estimates of the total number of men, women and children killed in the camp range from 300,000-700,000. While the majority of these were Serbs, there were also Jews and Romas, as well as anti-fascists of many nationalities (Simic 2014, p. 154). Olivera Simic in her memoir *Surviving Peace* states that the river Sava holds a special place in the memory of Serbs, and now I finally understood my grandfather's stories.

Each side was fighting their own war. The Chetniks waged a war against Bosnia's Croatian and Muslim citizens, tagging them with the label of Ustasha collaborators, and against the Partisans who they viewed as post-war rivals (Sacco 2018, p. 19). The Partisans were a predominantly Serb group, but as the war continued, they recruited a growing number of Muslim and Croatian recruits. The Partisans fought a two-pronged war, an offensive war against the Axis powers who occupied Yugoslavia and a campaign against the Chetniks, whom they crushed (Sacco 2018, pp. 20-22).

When WWII ended, Tito was left with a country full of tangled factions and loyalties, but the one uniting bond was Brotherhood and Unity under the yoke of communism. Ethnic loyalties were forbidden, the only loyalty was to the Communist party.

This worked until 1980 when Tito, the benevolent dictator, passed away without leaving a successor. In the aftermath, nationalist politicians with an eye to the future whipped up nationalist sentiments, using the convenient narrative of a fractured past to bolster their political ambitions.

In his seminal book *Bosnia: A short history,* Noel Malcom (1994) argues that:

> The main basis of hostility was not ethnic or religious but economic: the resentment felt by the members of a mainly (but not exclusively) Christian peasantry towards their Muslim landowners. This hostility was not some absolute or irreducible force: it varied as economic circumstances changed and was also subject to political pressures, which significantly altered the attitude of the landowning class during the first half of the nineteenth century. And the hostility between the Catholic and Orthodox communities was also subject to changing influences—rivalries between the Church hierarchies, political pressures from neighbouring countries, and so on (p. xxi).

Malcolm states that for most of the period after 1878, the different religious or ethnic communities in Bosnia lived peacefully together, and the exceptions were the two world wars which were caused and aggravated by causes outside of Bosnia's borders. After these episodes, two whole generations grew up who had "no personal memories of the fighting in that war, and no particular desire to revive it" (Malcolm 1994, p. xxi).

This is confirmed by Sacco who relates the story of Goražde resident Emir who states that "[m]y grandfather and grandmother sometimes tried to explain to me what happened during World War II, but I did not listen, or listened with one ear" (Sacco 2018, p. 23). While Simic (2014) notes that "[t]he Second World War was still a vivid memory for our parents and grandparents, although we had been taught about it at school, my generation had never actually experienced war" (p. 14).

In her book, *How Generations Remember: Conflicting histories and shared memories in post-war Bosnia and Herzegovina*, Monika Palmberger (2016) introduces the concept of "generational positioning, which incorporates age as well as stage of life (past and present)" (p. 3). She identifies the 'First Yugoslavs' as those who were born after WWII and predominantly lived during the period of socialist Yugoslavia (Palmberger 2016, p. 127). The 'Last Yugoslavs' who were "born and grew up in BiH during socialist Yugoslavia," after WWII and have no memories of the war or "first years of Tito's Yugoslavia" (Palmberger 2016, p. 165). And the 'post-Yugoslavs' who spent most of their lives in post-war than in pre-war time and grew up during the war (Palmberger 2016, p. 11). She clarifies that "the generations here are not political generations who share a politico-ideological outlook" but instead "each generation may be seen as a group of people who share a certain processing of experiences" (Palmberger 2016, p. 11).

There were many civilians who were ignorant of their religious identity by those who fall into the 'Last Yugoslavia' generation and to whom religion was not important at all. In her book, Leydesdorff (2011) interviewed Ćamila, a well-educated woman from Srebrenica, who is from a Muslim background who stated that:

> I never knew a person's religion, it wasn't important to me. We were just together, we walked, we sat together, we went out together. If I liked a boy, then I would look at him and giggle. Perhaps he made a remark or two, and that was that. That's how we got to know each other. We never made any distinction.

> We never thought about who was what. I didn't think
> it was important (p. 34).

This is echoed by Olivera Simic, who is of Serb origin and writes:

> I was unaware of my own ethnicity, and that of my
> family, until the time of Tito's death. One afternoon,
> in the spring of 1986, I came home from school and
> asked my father who I was. He did not understand
> my question. I explained that I had not been able to
> give an answer to my teacher when asked about my
> ethnic origin. My father said, "We are Serbs." As a
> thirteen-year-old I did not give a second thought to
> what my father told me that day (Simic 2014, p. 13).

This suggests that the shadow of WWII created distinct generational experiences of identity within Yugoslavia, entrenching the ethnic division in rural areas and removing them in urban areas.

Generational Identity and Urban-Rural Divide

When researching Srebrenica, I was once again struck by these same differences across urban/rural lines. In early March 1993, the Bosnian Serb Army, backed by troops and weapons from neighbouring Serbia, was threatening to take Srebrenica. Over 60,000 people had flooded into Srebrenica, a town that had a pre-war population of 9,000, from surrounding villages that had been ethnically cleansed and were exhausted, starving, and frightened (Rohde 2012, p. 45).

Emir Suljagić (2015) in *Postcards from the Grave* wrote a first-person account of his experience as a refugee who lived during the three-year siege of Srebrenica, and described how the residents during the siege spoke of Srebrenica as a ghetto or concentration camp. There was no barbed wire, watchtowers, or armed guards, however, the population was trapped by borders that were constantly shifting, "neither permanent nor stable, always moving to the advantage of the stronger party" (p. 25).

The residents were starving with Doctors without Borders reporting there were periods when the average daily calories consumed per person amounted to approximately 1,000, with the lowest point was in the autumn of 1994 (Leydesdorff 2011, p. 111). As the Serbs tightened the noose around Srebrenica and waged a campaign of terror through starvation, shelling and snipers, the population internally seethed with tension.

One of the most misunderstood aspects of Bosnian cultural identity by non-Bosnian authors is the schism between the urban and rural populations. This schism was a particularly Yugoslav issue because of the influence of communism and the effects it had on economic circumstances. The urban populations had greater education and gave up their religious beliefs in order to be members of the League of Communists and receive benefits and socialised across ethnic lines. The rural population was mostly uneducated, agrarian, old-fashioned in attitudes, practiced their religion and were outsiders from communist benefits, and were mostly segregated from other ethnicities.

In her memoir, Simic (1992) describes the experience of living under communism "[w]e coexisted only as part of a tribe and were raised to put the interests of our community and neighbours before our own" (p. xvi). While the communist ethos was about submerging individuality to be a part of the community, one schism still existed. Simic states "[w]e were divided along rural/urban lines—not along ethnic/religious ones" (Simic 1992, p. 12).

Yugoslavia was originally a land of peasants with 80% of the population living off the land in "old" pre-WWII Yugoslavia and yet by 1972 only 36% could be classified peasants and 60% industrial workers (Tomić-Koludrović, I. and Petrić, M. 2014). As socialism was introduced post WWII, there was rapid urbanisation and the need for bodies to work in these factories and there was a max exodus from rural areas to cities to become industrial workers (Tomić-Koludrović, I. and Petrić, M. 2014).

Yugoslavia's socialist economy was based on factory workers being "collective owners" of the factories, however, in practice, the real owners of collective ownership were those with the power to influence processes who became the new elite (Tomić-Koludrović, I. and Petrić, M. 2014). This new elite were the ones making the political decisions and their status was based on being insiders to the system and 90 percent of collective owners were League of Communist members. To be a communist meant to give up their religious loyalty and devotion in order to succeed (Tomić-Koludrović, I. and Petrić, M. 2014).

When looking at Bosnian census statistics for 1991, the year before the war began, "[t]he Republics of Croatia and Serbia, were dominated by Croat and Serb populations, respectively, but Bosnia and Herzegovina was mixed all three groups with approximately 44% of the population identifying themselves as Bosnian Muslim, 31% as Bosnian Serbs, and 17% as Bosnian Croat" (Ryan 2012, p. 7). In Srebrenica, however, that composition was very different and according to the last census conducted before the war, 73% percent described themselves as Muslims, 25% as Serbs, and 2 % as "Yugoslavs" or part of no ethnic group (Rohde 2012, p. XIV).

When examining the pre-war prejudices and tensions in Srebrenica hospital, Fink (2003) writes:

most of Srebrenica's doctors would later say that there had been little heat within the medical community until the day Bosnia held its own independence referendum in 1992. If anything, small conflicts flared between village folk and city slickers or between people from different towns such as less-developed Bratunac whose inhabitants were nicknamed 'frog-catchers' and Srebrenicans who were accused of snobbery and xenophobia and nicknamed 'storks' (p. 35).

Sudetić (1998) describes the difference between peasants and natives of Srebrenica as the natives spoke with a different dialect, danced the *kolo* (the traditional dance of the region) with different steps, and lived by different, less patient rhythms. Srebrenica people hopped into cars and drove to the cities of Belgrade or Sarajevo, while those in the villages would still have been crouching beside the general road, "smoking a third cigarette, and waiting for Unclo Avdo's friend to come bouncing along the cinder road in his beat-up local bus bound for Višegrad" (p. 138). The peasants had to emigrate, or a waste away in poverty, ignorance and alcoholism, while those in Srebrenica had employment to keep them close to home (Sudetić 1998, p. 138).

Many of those who were cleansed and poured into Srebrenica came from villages that dotted the mountains of eastern Srebrenica. Many of these villages were made of residents who all shared the same surname as their descendants "had settled there and multiplied and one day the family grew as numerous as a village" (Fink 2003, p. 38).

These villages had electricity connected and plumbing installed in the recent decade or two prior to the war, with women having to walk to wells to fetch water prior to that (Fink 2003, p. 38). The villagers were self-sufficient subsisting on the vegetables they grew, the sheep or cows they raised, and the women would spin wool and knit clothes. A high proportion was illiterate as schooling came second to household chores and children were kept at home.

A doctor mentioned by Fink in *War Hospital* named Ejub shared his life about growing up in one of these villages in 1959 and how attending school gave him a gateway to a world that was foreign to him. As he learned "about science and space and the race to put a man on the moon" from books, he found that the prayers he had to memorise at the mosque did not make sense. For Ejub, "The logic of science seemed to preclude the logic of religion so at age twelve he forsook religion and declared himself an atheist" (Fink 2003, p. 39). And his journey mirrors that of his peers, who became ever more educated and turned away from religion.

In the villages, there was greater homogeneity and, as a result, greater division between the Serb and Muslim population. Leydesdorff relates an anecdote from a former teacher the conflict about where a school should be built ten years before the war in Brežani; the village was half Serb and half Muslim, and the two parts of the village were six kilometres apart. The only solution was to build the school in the middle (Leydesdorff 2011, p. 32).

Even these villagers who were cleansed from their homes had more in common with each other than with the original residents of Srebrenica. They remained far from homogenous. Leydesdorff interviewed Sevda, a woman who lost male relatives to the genocide. When her parents opposed her marrying a young man from another village, Sevda ran away, only to learn she'd made a mistake. Her husband's family had a custom of eating from a communal pan instead of individual plates which she found uncivilised, and her husband beat her as he did his sisters (Leydesdorff 2011, p. 43).

Leydesdorff (2011) states that "World War II left its mark on the villages with memories being passed down" (p. 73). Šefika, a survivor of the Srebrenica siege, shares that she "had learned about hate from what her mother experienced in World War II. Her mother's first husband was suspected of belonging to the Croatian Ustaša and was killed by the partisans." However, Šefika herself lived in a touristy village on the Drina where she rented rooms and Muslims and Serbs lived together. Even though she had the memory of the WWII carnage, she lived an urban life in a vibrant city with other ethnicities and without prejudice (Leydesdorff 2011, p. 73).

While Hasanović (2016), a survivor of the Srebrenica massacre, relates a friendship across with his Serb neighbours because in WWII the Hasanović family had saved family members "by hiding them from the Ustaša soldiers in some furniture. Afterwards they became best friends, and that family was so grateful to my grandfather that they kept telling the story to their children" (p. 21)

Initially, when the Serbs attacked Srebrenica, the peasants in villages surrounding Srebrenica were spared and were able to continue working the fields. When starving Srebrenica residents hiked kilometres to reach villages to trade, villagers profiteered off desperate people who sold jewellery or used the last of their money for a little flour, a couple of eggs, a tiny bit of cheese. Sometimes they even said to the starving refugees "Why didn't you defend yourself?" (Suljagić 2015, p. 35).

When in March 1993 Serbs advanced on the borders, refugees from nearby villages arrived carrying everything they owned, on horse-drawn carts piled with all their belongings, whole families sitting on whatever belongings they could collect before running. Suljagić (2015) states, "[s]ome felt for them, others thought they got what they deserved" (p. 35).

As more villagers poured into Srebrenica, conditions deteriorated, with Hasnović (2016) relating that "in the beginning there was occasionally electricity and a little food as well, but soon refugees kept coming and moving into the houses and the flats. Soon the electricity was turned off, and we ran out of our food supplies as well" (p. 28). Initially, the arrival of the refugees who brought cattle provided meat as the cattle was slaughtered "[t]he town was full of both people and cattle and lots of noise" (Hasanović 2016, p. 28). Conditions deteriorated as some refugees couldn't find shelter and lived outside and as winter hit, they started "a fire by the asphalt on the side of the street" (Hasanović 2016, p. 32).

The Serbs were blocking convoys from entering, and the population was starving. A British doctor with the World Health Organisation who had trekked into Srebrenica through the mountains got word out that refugees were living in the streets, and the poorest were beginning to die of starvation (Rohde 2012, p. 45). Eventually Srebrenica was declared a safe zone by the United Nations and supposedly protected by NATO, but in effect the air support required to enact this was never deployed. The residents depended on United Nations convoys for food, which the Serbs blocked as they attempted to starve the population into submission.

In Srebrenica, control was in the hands of the original residents, who had more access to relief supplies. That control was tainted by internal visions and power struggles between council members who belonged to a new Muslim elite that had acquired political power in the years before the war (Leydesdorff 2011, p. 111).

The town's original inhabitants tried to bathe and stay clean to lead relatively normal lives. "They looked down on the refugees who lived from hand to mouth, didn't bathe every day, stole, and suddenly had become very religious. The refugees (especially the women) were less educated. They were less 'civilised'" (Leydesdorff 2011, p. 111).

As hygiene deteriorated, there were infestations of lice and scabies, which further stigmatised the refugees, (Fink 2003, p. 206). This prejudice was confirmed when typhoid medicine was airdropped by the US near villagers who viewed everything that they didn't understand as a threat. When they found the typhoid medicine and "not knowing what they were, tossed them into a fire" (Fink 2003, p.154)

Suljagić (2015) writes about corruption in the besieged town and describes the two tiers of society within the enclave with the President of the Municipal council showing off cardboard packs of Marlboro bought from Canadian and Dutch soldiers while Suljagić and his friends made cigarettes out of paper and bitter home-grown tobacco that pinched the throat and burned into black ashes. And some municipal-council officials drove in cars while refugees walked dozens of kilometres wearing bad shoes (p. 30-31).

While Mangafić and Veselinović (2020) explore corruption after the Balkan conflict, their study provides some insight in relation to Srebrenica that further emphasises the divide between rural and urban residents. In their research they found that "corruption is a widespread phenomenon in Bosnia-Herzegovina, and more educated people, people living in urban areas, and individuals with higher incomes are more likely to engage in bribery in several sectors" (p. 2670). The factors that led to the division of residents in Srebrenica into the haves and have nots were also divisions within those who were more educated and had more access to resources and influence, and that the divisions between the rural and urban population contributed to the distribution of resources.

While the original residents found the refugees 'uncivilised', they also had use for them. They were used by the Bosnian government as a bargaining chip to maintain Srebrenica as a haven, protected by UN forces. Whenever a convoy arrived with food relief, desperate refugees swarmed the empty trucks in order to leave Srebrenica, until eventually even this escape was blocked. "If the evacuations from Srebrenica continued at this rate, there would soon be no substantial civilian population left" (Honig and Both, 1996, p. 92). They were concerned that if there were no civilians whose lives were directly under threat, then the pressure to save those left behind would subside (Honig and Both, 1996, p. 92).

They were also used to boost troop numbers during 'actions,' which is what military engagements were called in the area. Fink called them *hapsi*, as they were the HPO division. Fink (2003) states that the "H" stands for *hapsi*, a Bosnian word for petty thieves. She describes them during an action "as thousands upon thousands of civilians pour in, like a lava flow, to pillage Serb villages. By their sheer numbers and the thunder of their voices the howling, bag-carrying hordes help scare Serb inhabitants away" (p. 101).

While Suljagić (2015 p. 52-55) and Sudetić (Sudetić 1998, p. 157) called these troops *torbari*, so named after the bags they carried to collect their stolen plunder. The civilians were desperate and starving and would accompany the soldiers on actions. By the end of the first year, there were more civilians than soldiers. The *torbari* would wait for the first bunker to fall, or first Serb soldiers to start running way, and run after them, screaming, banging on pots, screaming "Allahu-ekber!" to scare the Serbs and create the impression of Bosnian superiority. Civilians perished in greater numbers than soldiers, as those who were starving and wanting an extra piece of food would run into crossfire (Suljagić 2015, p. 52-55). Regardless of their name, they were the shield used to protect Srebrenica.

This highlights that the factors that led to the division of residents in Srebrenica into the haves and have nots were also divisions within those who were more educated and had more access to resources and influence, and that the divisions between the rural and urban population contributed to the distribution of resources.

The urban/rural divide played a part in the way the two Bosniak populations interacted. Initially, the rural population was at an advantage, safe and protected in the hills, while the urban population suffered attacks and deprivation and struggled for food. When the Chetniks cleared the villagers and they were made refugees, then they were at a disadvantage in the urban population where the elite controlled resources and exploited them by keeping them trapped and using them to bulk up their numbers as they were attacked by the enemy. Even though these were one people, they firmly viewed themselves as two distinct groups and all their interactions were predicated on this.

Yugoslav Muslim

While Yugoslavia was a socialist country in the latter years before the Bosnian War, it was originally predicated on the Russian communist principles where religion was to be submerged, and the new identity of Yugoslav was born. This is reflected in the first post-war census that was taken in 1948 and 'Moslem' "was considered a religious rather than an ethnic category" (Botev 1994). As a result, any residents who declared themselves as "Moslems also had to identify themselves as belonging to one of the large nationalities and were registered as "Serb-Moslem," "Croat-Moslem," and so on." This changed in the 1953 census when "the "Moslem" category was abolished, and Moslems of Yugoslav ethnic origin were classified as "Yugoslav-undeclared," and it was only 1961 that the census included the category "ethnic Moslem" (Botev 1994, p. 463).

Amra Sabic-El-Rayess (2023) in her chapter in *Bosnian Studies* also touches on this and explores the effects of this marginalisation of Muslim identity and how it "symbolised inferiority and subservience to other recognised ethnic groups and identities, often manifesting through literature and educational practices, content, and pedagogies" (p. 125). She argues that the underrepresentation of Bosniaks and other minorities was the norm, and it was a "structural and intentional discriminatory" act and that "the history, culture and language of Serbs—the dominant ethnic group to the constructed Yugoslavia—were positioned in curricula as central to the cornerstone of the constructed Yugoslav identity" (Sabic-El-Rayess, 2023, p. 126). I can confirm this from my experience from living in Yugosloavia between 1985 and 1989 and attending the secondary school where the language we spoke and were taught in was called Srpsko-Hrvatski, which means Serbo-Croat language, which underlines the marginalisation of Bosnian culture and identity. Furthermore, each week we alternated reading and writing the Cyrillic and Latin alphabet.

This highlights the injustice in how Muslim identity was viewed within Yugoslavia demonstrates the Islamophobia at work for centuries that led to the conflict, and the way that only those who were in rural areas and did not rely on communist benefits were able to openly practice their religion and identity as Muslims.

The post-Yugoslav Muslim

As the ethnic cleansing continued and those in Srebrenica found ways to cope and survive, school was reinstated and one of the new subjects introduced was religion. One of the women interviewed by Leydesdorff (2011) describes her experience of attending to school and not even knowing she was a Muslim before this, "[s]uddenly I had to learn all about it, including Arabic and reading the Qur'an"

(p. 137). When the Iman asked who didn't know how to pray, she and another original Srebrenicians resident raised their hand. "Many of the kids came from the villages, where belief was more common, so they had learnt all that from their parents. My parents still don't know anything about that, so how could I have known?" (Leydesdorff 2011, p. 137). The Iman chastises her because her parents did not teach her anything.

As the persecution of Bosniaks occurred, there was a repositioning of identity within the community. Those who did not think of themselves as Muslim or were practicing were now confronted with being murdered for something that they did not have any control over.

This illustrates a broader socio-political trend occurring within Bosniaks who were not religious before, finding strength in their faith, and repositioning their identity away from the socialist ideals they had embraced and been betrayed for. So, while only Bosniaks in rural populations within what was Yugoslavia did practice the five pillars of Islam which were:

Shahadah: the declaration of faith.

Salah: praying five times each day.

Zakat: giving money to charity or those in need.

Sawm: fasting during the month of Ramadan.

Hajj: pilgrimage to Mecca.

Those Bosniaks in urban populations did have cultural practices embedded within their lives which were to not eat pork, circumcise males, give their children Muslim names that had Arabic and Turkish origins, and drink Turkish coffee.

Muslims avoided eating pork due to religious dietary restrictions outlined in Islamic teachings. In Islam, consuming pork is considered haram (forbidden) as it is explicitly prohibited in the Quran, the holy book of Islam. The prohibition is based on verses that emphasise cleanliness, health, and obedience to God's commands. Pork is believed to be impure, and its consumption is discouraged to maintain spiritual and physical well-being in accordance with Islamic principles. This dietary restriction is a significant aspect of Islamic dietary laws and is followed by Muslims as a religious obligation.

The shadow of WWII remained more dominant in the rural populations and created a greater separation between Bosniak populations and those of other religious affiliations, while in the city, the memories of war were submerged and erased and there was greater coexistence and unity.

The urban-rural divide in Yugoslavia was not simply a cultural or geographic difference—it was a profound fault line that shaped personal identity, access to power, and community resilience. In examining Srebrenica, we see how this division influenced every layer of survival, solidarity, and suffering. Urban residents, often more secular, educated, and politically connected, held influence over resources and external networks, while rural populations—more religious, traditional, and economically marginalised—bore the brunt of both displacement and social exclusion within the enclave. This internal fracture mirrored the broader collapse of Yugoslav ideals like Brotherhood and Unity, revealing how superficial that unity had become under the weight of economic inequity and suppressed ethnic memory. Understanding this divide is crucial not just for historical accuracy, but for honouring the layered trauma of survivors and reckoning with how memory is formed, preserved, or denied. Only by acknowledging these internal complexities can we move toward genuine reconciliation and ensure such fractures are not repeated in future conflicts.

Bosnia as a pluralist society

The war in Bosnia is a religious war that was brought about by Islamophobia to destroy a centuries old-pluralist society, which goes against the historical narrative that this was a civil war. In fact, the Muslim community under the Ottoman empire was tolerant and accepting and allowed religious harmony to flourish, and this needed to be distorted to fan the flames of Islamophobia and breed nationalism.

Pluralism, in this context, typically means a society or political system that recognises and respects the coexistence of diverse groups, such as different ethnicities, religions, or cultural identities. During the Ottoman Empire, Bosnia was a pluralist society and acceptance of diversity was a defining characteristic of Bosnia for many generations.

Bosnia was an independent kingdom from 1377 to 1463, and Islam arrived under Ottoman imperialism 1463 to 1878. Before Islam and the Ottomans in 1463, there were three religions during the Middle Ages that were all battling for followers: Roman Catholicism, Serbian Orthodoxy and the Bosnian Church (Zilic 1998, p. 15).

Yugoslav socialist views promoted that the teaching of the Bosnian Church was heretic, however Malcolm (1994) states that most of the evidence pointing to it being heretic come out of Bosnia itself (p. 31), and believes that it was most likely "a monastic organisation based on the rule of St Basil" and "must have been founded by people from the Eastern tradition" (pp 35-36).

When my grandfather explained to me our religious heritage, he stated we had our own Bosnian Church, and we converted to Islam because it was like our beliefs, which was a claim promoted by twentieth-century Muslims "to counter Catholic-Croat or Orthodox-Serb claims that the Muslims are really Croats, or Serbs, who apostasised to Islam and should return to their true religious origins" (Zilic 1998, p. 16). However, modern scholarship has disproven this theory and shown that there are many reasons for the mass conversions to Islam.

By the time that the Ottoman Empire arrived, the Bosnian Church was waning, and Islamisation of Bosnia took place over 150 years (Malcolm 1994, p. 54). Some reasons for conversation is that in "country areas poorly served by priests, Christianity (in whatever form) had probably become little more than a set of folk practices and ceremonies" and as a result the "shift from folk Christianity to folk Islam was not very great; many of the same practices could continue albeit with slightly different words or names" (Malcolm 1994, p. 58). The privileged legal status of Muslims (Malcolm 1994, p. 66) and "slavery and the growth of Muslim towns" (Malcolm 1994, p. 66) which is the standard Ottoman practice of taking of slaves who could then gain their freedom by becoming Muslims so that in "1528 these freed slaves made up nearly 8 percent of the entire population of Sarajevo" (Malcolm 1994, p. 67). And also, the "influx of already Islamised Slavs from outside of Bosnia's borders" (Malcolm 1994, p. 68) as the Ottoman empire retreated and they sought refuge.

Most Islamisation was not a result of forced conversions, and the Ottoman empire showed great tolerance and acceptance of other religions. They even offered asylum to the expelled Jews of al-Andalus from Spain, who found refuge in Sarajevo. As a result, Sarajevo was called the Little Jerusalem of the Jewish world because it was the only other city apart from Jerusalem where you could find a "mosque, a Catholic cathedral, an Orthodox church and a synagogue" within a few hundred square metres (Zilic 1998, p. 15). Or in Gautman's (1993a) words, "Sarajevo, with its skyline of minarets, church steeples and synagogues, was testimony to centuries of civilised multiethnic coexistence" (p. xix).

And while "it is true that Christians (and Jews) were not full co-equals with the Muslim subjects of the Ottomans" they did enjoy a "far greater equality than any minorities in Christian Europe" as they had "their own courts" to resolve their own civil cases and also "large measure of religious freedom" (Zilic 1998, P. 17).

To sum up, the Ottoman Empire allowed its minorities to practice their own religion and have rights as citizens, and conversions to Islam were mostly for the benefits they gained under Ottoman rule, and this tolerance further continued under the next empire that controlled Bosnia. When the Ottoman Empire annexed Bosnia to the Austro-Hungarian empire in 1879, they were faced with the "delicate task" of how to handle "the three main religious communities" (Malcolm 1994, p. 144).

They did this by establishing "a political system which recognised and reproduced diversity, and, in principle, awarded all nationalities and local languages equal rights" (Sluga 2001, p. 210). They gained cooperation and control by subsidising religious schools and controlling "the appointment of the senior figures in each religious group" (Malcolm 1994, p. 144). The authorities were "conscious of the danger" in privileging the Bosnian Catholics who shared the same religious background as them (Malcolm 1994, p. 145).

When the American journalist W.E. Curtis visited Bosnian in 1902, he witnessed:

> Members of the different religious faiths mix with each other on amicable terms to show mutual respect and mutual toleration; the courts are wisely and honestly administered, justice is awarded to every citizen, regardless of his religion or social position (Malcolm 1994, p. 145).

Malcolm (1994) supports this view of Bosnian history and states that for most of the time after 1878, "the different religious or ethnic communities in Bosnia lived peacefully together" (p. xxi) and these were only interrupted by the two world wars. These wars were "induced and aggravated by causes outside Bosnia's borders" and after WWII "two whole generations" had grown up and "no personal memories" of the war and "no particular desire to revive it" (Malcolm 1994, P xxi).

Ahmed Zilic (1998) calls Bosnia "the symbolic Jerusalem of the new world order" and states that "on the basis of their historical, anthropological, political and cultural background, the two million Muslims in Bosnia and Herzegovina are authentic Europeans" (p. 22). The Bosnians, as "European people" were "discriminated against" with "war crimes and genocidal acts" because "of their different religion." He further continues this metaphor of Bosnia as a symbolic Jerusalem when he ends that "the walls of this Jerusalem fell in Srebrenica, breached by new quasi-Crusader" (Zilic 1998, p. 22).

This indicates Bosnia was a multiethnic society for centuries and citizens lived in harmony with each other. So how and why did this change? This change in society occurred as a result of ultranationalists uniting in Islamophobia.

The goal of the ultranationalists was to destroy "Bosnia as it had existed for six centuries" as a multiethnic and multi-religious region, where Muslims, Serbs, Croats, and others had lived together for centuries. The different ethnic communities were now being pitted against each other so that multiculturalism as "the fabric which wove the lives of its many peoples together [was] torn beyond repair" (Ali and Lifschultz, 1994, p. 367) in order to ensure each ethnic community only proclaimed their own self-interest and loyalty to their own ethnicity.

The way to do this was to terrorise the "native Muslim population" so that they were cleansed out of these desired territories and to destroy the dangerous "cosmopolitanism of its cities" (Ali and Lifschultz, 1994, p. 367) which demonstrated the coexistence of multiple ethnic groups. Within this fantasy then "a 'cleansed' Bosnia could then be carved up and annexed" (Ali and Lifschultz, 1994, p. 367). So, once Bosnia's identity as a distinct, multiethnic state was destroyed, it would be divided between 'Greater Serbia' and 'Greater Croatia' and annexed into ethnically homogeneous states.

Propaganda was used to ignite and justify aggression by "[b]oth Serbian and Croatian academics, journalists, military leaders and politicians" that was focused on "the fear of Islamic expansion and violence to legitimate their own nationalist expansion and violence" (MacDonald 2003, pp. 239-240). Both Serbs and Croats "ran 'detention centres' and 'collection camps' where prisoners were housed, fed little to no food, frequently beaten and terrorised, sometimes sexually violated, and often killed" (MacDonald 2003, pp. 239-240). The largest were Serb-controlled 13 major camps, while the Croats maintained 4 camps, however "[t]he International Red Cross, by August 1994, had documented a total of 51, many small and impromptu—located in camp grounds, schools, even movie theatres" (MacDonald 2003, pp. 239-240).

But this was not enough. They needed to turn their own population into supporters of their own agenda to genocide. They had to do this by "gradually implicating the Bosnian Serb community in their project of aggression and expansion" (Ali and Lifschultz, 1994, p. 376). This was a slow process of first isolating any Serbs who opposed their plans and then implicating "all the others in what initially were small acts of repression against the other communities and, ultimately, in very large and horrid crimes" (Ali and Lifschultz, 1994, p. 376).

Bosnia was a multiethnic society for centuries and it was betrayed by ultranationalists who promoted their own interests for a land grab by destroying the foundations of this society.

Uniting under the flag of Islamophobia

Foundational myths were used to unite ultranationalists against Bosniaks using Islamophobia. Serbs were united under symbols of religious intolerance and this rhetoric was used to create a tear in Bosnian society and end religious harmony.

When looking at how Slobodan Milošević promoted nationalism and the war, he used the Battle of Kosovo as a unifying myth. This battle has been mythologised in Serbian epic poetry and nationalist narratives and has become a symbolic event that represents the heroism and sacrifice of Serbs who faced "cataclysmic defeat" in the face of the advancing Ottoman Empire. According to myth, the noble warriors who fought are "the flower of Balkan chivalry" who died defending Serbia from the Ottomans, symbolising a tragic loss of the Serbian elite and national identity (Malcolm 1994, p. 20). While there were heavy losses on both sides and Prince Lazar was captured and killed, and "[i]t was not the battle itself" that led to fall of Serbia, but that Turks returned "year after year, in ever increasing strength" so that "by 1392 all the Serbian Orthodox lands, apart from Bosnian-ruled Hum, had submitted to Ottoman suzerainty" (Malcolm 1994, p. 20). The myth portrays this as the last stand of Serb nationhood.

Milošević used this anniversary on 28 June 1989 to assemble "several hundred thousand Serbs" at the battlefield Gazimestan (Malcolm 1994, p. 213). He had begun his nationalist mythmaking with the bones of Prince Lazar touring the country and becoming an object of pilgrimage and in the courtyard of the monastery while people "queued to pay devotion to the Prince's bones inside, stalls sold icon-style posters of Jesus Chris, Prince Lazar and Slobodan Milošević side by side" (Malcolm 1994, p. 213). Prince Lazar is viewed as a symbol of martyrdom and heroism, while Jesus Christ is divine authority, so with the use of this iconography Milošević was elevating himself to a similar status as one who is a leader chosen by destiny to be a protector of the nation.

On the backdrop behind him he had the Serb nationalist emblem "an Orthodox cross with a Cyrlic C (equivalent to Latin S) at each of the four corners of the cross. The CCCC symbol stands for the slogan "Only Unity Saves the Serb" (*Samo sloga Srbina Spašava*) (Sells 1996, p. 86). As he began his speech about "not armed battles yet, though it may come to that" the meaning of unity was defined as the unity of Serbs "against all others" (Sells 1996, p. 87).

The war was flown under the banner of a religious war whose purpose was to destroy pluralism and religious harmony, and past violences of the Ottoman invasion were used to influence the present.

Ultranationalists used "myths disguised as history" in order "to breed fear and insecurity among Serbs wherever they lived" and cultivated "group paranoia" so that "the Muslims of Bosnia suddenly became the enemy within" (Ali and Lifschultz, 1994, p. 376). One of the myths was that their Bosnian neighbours:

> were converted into the conquering Turks of the Middle Ages who had occupied 'Serb' lands and oppressed the Serb nation. This vision of the Ottoman Turk was fused with a caricature of Islamic 'Mujahideen' descending on the Balkans intent on establishing a terrorist state in Bosnia (Ali and Lifschultz, 1994, p. 376).

Through this ideology, Serbia was acting in 'self-defence' and the "war became Christianity's last stand against Islamic hegemony over Europe" (Ali and Lifschultz, 1994, p. 376). And so, they were framing this as not just a civil war but a religious war in which they were protecting the survival of Christianity in Europe. Therefore, their actions were heroic and righteous, as they were stopping the Muslim dominance and "were fighting the last Crusade" (Ali and Lifschultz, 1994, p. 376).

Sells (1996) argues it was repeatedly denied "that it was religiously motivated and religious justified" and that "[r]eligious symbols, mythologies, myths of origin (pure Serb race), symbols of passion (Lazar's death), and the eschatological longings (the resurrection of Lazar) were used by religious nationalists" and it was used not only in speeches and manifesto, but in "specific rituals of atrocity" (p. 89).

The international community supports Islamophobia

The myth of the Balkan Conflict of 1992-1995 being a civil war was used to support international inaction and, as a result, the international intervention became complicit in the suffering of Bosnia's people.

Rabia Ali and Lawrence Lifschultz (1994) state that the UN contributed to ending a multiethnic life because "A UN-imposed arms embargo guaranteed that a well-armed Serbia could annex territory and expel over a million civilians while facing only limited resistance" (p. 369). The international community "first recognised Bosnia as a sovereign and independent state" (Zilic 1998, P. 21). Though this act they "exposed its cynicism and openly made concessions to the Belgrade regime, which was heavily armed, while preventing the unarmed defenders of Bosnia from obtaining arms and defending themselves" (Zilic 1998, P. 21). Because of the embargo, the Muslim forces were the weakest and were "largely fighting a war of self-defence" (MacDonald 2003, P. 255).

While the international community attempted to paint this as a civil war, "war, however, is a conflict between armed adversaries" (Sells 1996, p. 117). Due to the embargo, the Bosniaks did not have the ability to fight on an equal ground and "the Serb army took towns and villages that lacked significant military defences" (Sells 1996, p. 117). If a Bosnian town happened to have any defence, then the "Serb militants used heavy artillery to shell the defenders into submission" (Sells 1996, p. 117). As a result, Sells (1996) argues that "[t]his was not war but organised destruction of a largely unarmed population" (p. 117).

The embargo did disadvantage the Bosniak population and advantaged the Serb aggressor, but this was not enough to enable the Serb atrocities. Western inaction and their own propaganda minimising the conflict and representing this as a civil war was also to blame.

The United Nations sided and supported this myth from within its own ranks. Lewis MacKenzie, a Canadian army general, chief of staff of the United Nations peacekeeping force, who left under controversial circumstances when accusations were made, was aware of UN peacekeepers visiting and taking "sexual advantage of Muslim and Croat women forced into prostitution" (Gutman 1993b).

MacKenzie had undertaken "a speaking tour funded by Serbian American advocacy group" whose mission was to "dispel the internationally accepted view that Serb fighters were principally responsible for the mass killings, rape and 'ethnic cleaning' that have destroyed the former Yugoslav republic" (Gutman 1993a, p. 168).

In a testimony before the House of Armed Services Committee, MacKenzie argued "that all the parties in the Balkan war are to blame for atrocities" and that all sides are "serial killers" (Gutman 1993a, p. 169). This statement is in dispute by "the State Department's own reports listing 285 instances of war crimes, of which only 18 involved actions by Muslim forces" (Gutman 1993a, p. 169). During his public appearances he has also often made the statement that the "vast majority of ceasefire violations that he observed in Bosnia were committed by the predominantly Muslim government forces" even though other "UN officers who served with him say that the assertion distorts the facts" (Gutman 1993a, p. 170).

As an "authoritative and believable figure" (Gutman 1993, p. 171), MacKenzie was the perfect mouthpiece for Serb propaganda and did much to undermine the reality on the ground of Serb atrocities being committed. A reality that was known to UN officials, according to Louis Gentile, who was the UN High Commission for Refugees and stated "the so-called leaders of the Western world have known for the past year and a half what is happening here. They receive play-by-play reports" (Sells 1996, p. 115). Gentile ends his statement with the lament "[m]ay God forgive them, may God forgive us all" (Sells 1996, p. 115) demonstrating that he finds the Western world, and the UN of which he is a part of, culpable of atrocities in Bosnia as they did nothing to intervene and stop the war crimes.

The false realities were presented that "the conflict as a civil war in which all sides were, more or less, guilty; a war in which there were no principles or ideals worth defending, or identifying with" (Ali and Lifschultz, 1994, p. 370).

Gutman (1993a) argues that it was the US who put this position forward as a way of justifying the fact that their inaction in the war. He traces this to the publication of a Newsday article in August 1992 that included "eyewitness accounts of systemised murder in concentration camps" (p. xviii). In response to this, "Bush expressed shock" and incorrectly described the war "as a blood feud arising from ancient animosities." Gutman (1993) concludes that "[t]o justify his inaction, Bush revised history" (p. xviii).

This is confirmed by Tone Bringa (2002) who states that "[t]o many policy makers in Europe and the United States it was convenient to describe what was going on as 'ethnic cleansing' because if they were to acknowledge it as genocide then there might be "a legal obligation to intervene, either to prevent genocide from happening or to stop it while in progress" (p. 203).

There was a need to 'other' Bosnia and its population so that they were "unlike other, more 'western', societies" and that the war was a "product of centuries-old enmities between the Serbs, Croats, and Muslims" (Ali and Lifschultz, 1994, p. 370) so was the result of long-standing, historical hostilities between these ethnic groups. This was a "tribal blood-feud" (Ali and Lifschultz, 1994, p. 370) implying that it was primitive and based on revenge or irrational hatred in order to reduce the complexity of the war to a simplistic, violent clash between groups. As a "'typical' Balkan convulsion" (Ali and Lifschultz, 1994, p. 370) reinforcing a stereotype that the region is prone to these periodic eruptions of violence and that these conflicts were common in the Balkans due to its history, culture, or ethnic composition. As a result, this war could "not be understood much less mediated by any intervention by the civilised world" (Ali and Lifschultz, 1994, p. 370).

Gutman (1993a) concludes that while "Milosević takes most of the blame for what followed, it is hard to see how he could have launched a series of wars without the acquiescence of the United States and Western Europe" (p. xxiv).

The Western world and international organisations did not just hobble the Bosniak population from being able to defend themselves but actually promoted the inaccurate reality that this was a civil war that all parties were responsible for and spread misinformation and propaganda that the Muslims were breaking the ceasefire. This highlights how Islamophobia played a part in the failure to prevent the atrocities committed under the eyes of the West.

The role of intermarriage within what was Yugoslavia

One of the myths that is put forward about the former Yugoslavia is that intermarriage played a role within the social cohesion of the country. Petrović (2024) states that "intermarriage rates were not uniform across the country, indicating persistent ethnic divisions despite efforts towards national integration." And that "[t]hese marriages were seen as a tool to overcome historical ethnic divisions and create a cohesive Yugoslav identity" (as cited in Lendák-Kabók 2024). This illustrates that there was a goal in presenting this myth to the masses to confirm and consolidate the Yugoslav identity, however research does not confirm there were enough instances of intermarriage within the population to actually demonstrate the national integration that was much desired by the Communist government.

What is often overlooked within this myth of intermarriage and its influence on a shared Yugoslav identity is the role of religion and that fact that "ethnic identities in Yugoslavia are strongly associated with religion" (Kukić 2023) and as a result this religious association was a key marker of ethnic distinction. Kukić (2003) further states that "ethnic fractionalisation decreased religious prejudice, and made religion less important in shaping individual behaviour," so in regions with more ethnic diversity, there may have been less religious prejudice because people of different ethnic (and religious) backgrounds would interact more, making religion less critical in shaping their individual behaviour (Kukić 2023).

Because of this "tight association between religion and ethnicity" those who were less religious or secular "might have in turn" experienced "decreased ethnic nationalism, stimulating Yugoslav sentiment" (Kukić 2023). So, this decline in religious expression could have encouraged a broader Yugoslav identity, transcending ethnic and religious divisions. This interpretation is backed by a study from Kunovich and Hodson (2002), which found that religiosity (strong religious beliefs) was the most significant factor contributing to ethnic prejudice in Bosnia and Herzegovina (as cited in Kukić 2023).

Therefore, Leonard Kukić suggests that in Yugoslavia, increased ethnic diversity could have led to a reduction in religious and ethnic divisions, which fostered a greater sense of unity under a Yugoslav identity. As a result, intermarriage was only practiced by those who were less religious and viewed themselves more as secular Yugoslavs.

This is important as the division between Yugoslav society was between the urban population who had greater education and gave up their religious beliefs in order to be members of the League of Communists and receive benefits and socialised across ethnic lines. This is confirmed by Sekulić (1994) who found "that the self-declared Yugoslavs were the urban residents, the young, the better educated, ethnic minorities, and the Communist Party members" (as cited in Kukić 2023). While the rural population was mostly uneducated, agrarian, old-fashioned in attitudes, practiced their religion and were outsiders from communist benefits, and were mostly segregated from other ethnicities.

Within this context, it makes sense that "that interethnic marriages were more frequent in urban and industrialised areas where different ethnic groups" lived together and interacted in "workplaces, schools, and community centres" (as cited by Cvitković in Lendák-Kabók 2024). Within these social settings, "the importance of ethnic identity was often diminished in favour of a shared Yugoslav identity" and so this is what led to higher rates of interethnic marriage" (as cited by Cvitković in Lendák-Kabók 2024). In conclusion, there was more intermarriage within the urban population that was less connected to religion, while intermarriage was frowned upon within the rural population.

The other factor that influenced intermarriage was the cultural differences between different ethnic groups. As a result, "religious disparities also played a significant role in intermarriage decisions, with differences between Orthodox Christianity, Islam, and Catholicism significantly influencing marital choices (as cited by Burić and Petrović in Lendák-Kabók 2024).

These ethnicities are influenced by the different occupations of what was Yugoslavia over the past few centuries, so the "predominantly Catholic" Slovenes and Croats existed under 'Western' cultural tradition' during the Austro-Hungarian empire. While Serbs, Montenegrins and Macedonians, who are mostly Eastern Orthodox, embodied a 'near-Eastern' cultural tradition' within the former Ottoman Empire. And the Albanians and Bosniak Muslim populations were "within a 'Middle Eastern' cultural milieu" (as cited by Botev and Wagner in Lendák-Kabók 2024).

A study using data from the 1981 Yugoslav Census (Savezni Zavod za Statistiku, 1991) and the Yugoslav population administration (Savezni Zavod za Statistiku, 1963, 1974, 1982, 1990) found that "only for two of the eight ethnic groups studied, the proportion of mixed marriages in 1981 was more than 10%" (Smits, 2010). These two groups were small and thus did not significantly impact the total number of mixed marriages in the country. It also found that "social closure was strongest among Albanians and Muslims" (Smits 2010).

Social closure describes how ethnic groups restrict or limit relationships, such as marriage, with individuals from outside their group to maintain distinct boundaries and identities. Here, Albanians and Muslims exhibited the highest levels of social closure in terms of marriage. The data from 1981 shows that only 1.8% of Albanians and 3.5% of Muslims who were married had a spouse from a different ethnic background. This implies that both groups primarily married within their own ethnic communities, suggesting strong social boundaries and a preference for endogamy (marrying within one's group).

Speaking from personal experience when I wrote in The Age about my mother threatening to disinherit me if I married someone from another faith:

> I [come] from a family where marrying into the same religion mattered. My grandfather had moved my grandmother and his children from Croatia where he had stable work, back to Bosnia where his family was plunged into poverty, because his daughters were of marrying age, and they were flirting with Croatian Catholics. When he lay on his deathbed, he summoned his unattached grandchildren and made them promise they would marry into the Muslim faith. Only one of six did not comply. The rest of us bowed to his will (Pajalic 2023).

This indicates that intermarriage was only more prevalent in those who were not religious, which usually only happened when there was a proximity in cultural understanding, eg. Middle Eastern versus Western tradition. Statistics support that intermarriage was not as common as the Communist authorities led the public and the international community to believe. Those who were of Muslim background had much lower rates and acceptance of intermarriage.

When looking at depictions of intermarriage as being a key characteristic of Yugoslav society, this creates a misleading impression of Bosnian society before the genocide in Srebrenica. By highlighting intermarriage as a form of social cohesion, there is the risk of reinforcing the perception that the Bosnian War was a civil war among closely intertwined communities. This is problematic because it obscures the specific, targeted violence of genocide in Srebrenica, where Bosniak Muslims were systematically persecuted in an effort to lay claim to this mineral rich enclave. Although intermarriage existed, it was not a defining factor of Srebrenica's social fabric nor a significant point of unity that could counterbalance ethnic tensions.

There is some debate about the rise of intermarriage within Yugoslavia's Communist period, with some stating this was more dominant in urban areas and rare in rural areas. This is confirmed by Leydesdorff, who reports that "mixed marriages were more common" in Sarajevo and that other sources confirm that "there were few marriages between Muslims and other groups. ... but there is no hard data for East Bosnia" (Leydesdorff 2011, p. 31).

In his detailed study of intermarriage in Yugoslavia, Nikolai Botev (1994) interrogates the belief "that ethnic exogamy in Yugoslavia has been increasing" and is one of the reasons that leads to social integration (p. 464). Exogamy refers to the social practice of marrying outside one's specific social group, clan, or tribe, so whether those who are from the former Yugoslav republics of Bosnia and Herzegovina, Croatia, Serbia, Macedonia, Albania, Slovenia, and Montenegro were marrying outside of their own ethnic group. While Botev (1994) identifies one of the most serious limitations of his data is that "the definitions of some of the ethnic groups have varied over time" as there was "pressure from the authorities for ethnic assimilation and to other specific circumstances" (p. 465). Ultimately, he concluded that the "data indicates no clear upward trend in the proportion of mixed marriages" and that "according to marriage registration data, between 12 and 13 percent of marriages in Yugoslavia as a whole are mixed, with little variation over time" (Botev 1994, p. 468).

While he states that there are indications that in the large urban cities, intermarriage among the three groups Bosnian, Croatian and Serb, are more prevalent, however the data that he used in his study did not give him the opportunity to verify this. He did, however, conclude that there is "considerable regional variation in Yugoslavia: In Kosovo the proportion of exogamous marriages declined from 9.4 in 1962 to 1964 to only 4.7 percent in 1987 to 1989; during the same period, the percentage of mixed marriages in Vojvodina increased from 22.5 to 28.4" (Botev 1994, p. 468). As a result, this data suggests that intermarriage rates vary significantly from one region to another within the former Yugoslavia and that where people lived in the former Yugoslavia played a bigger role in determining rates of ethnic intermarriage than when they lived.

Botev (1994) found that:

> On the basis of marriage registration data and using log-linear models to characterise associations and differential change, I have found this notion to be an exaggeration. Rather, ethnic endogamy has been the

norm in Yugoslavia, and over the years studied (1962 to 1989) no clear trend emerged, either in terms of increasing rates of intermarriage or decreasing social distance between the various ethnic groups and cultural traditions (p. 476).

Essentially, Botev found that this belief that mixed marriages were more common in cities such as Sarajevo was not supported by data.

While Botev (1994) notes that:

The conventional sociological wisdom that intermarriage is an indicator of social integration remains intact, however, at least in this case, judging from the levels of ethnic endogamy, Yugoslavia has never been fully integrated: Thus, there is no mystery in that country's disintegration, although the violence accompanying the disintegration remains profoundly disturbing (p. 477).

So Botev, through his comprehensive study and by combing through other studies and data on intermarriage found that overall while this idea that intermarriage is a form of social cohesion that is present in other countries, it was never a true marker of integration in Yugoslavia and as a result it is no surprise that the country that was once Yugoslavia, has now disintegrated into separate and independent countries with their own cultural and religious identities.

Women in war

There are many stories of women and their role in the war that are overlooked and missing from the narrative. Leydesdorff (2011) interviewed Nezira who was on the front line with her sons and said that there were many other women there, presumably to take care of their menfolk. While on the front she was "a cook, a nurse…I did whatever and went everywhere to protect my children" (Leydesdorff 2011, p. 165). She describes her transformation from the horror and injuries she saw, and the sight of blood doesn't concern her at all. She states that "I didn't take my boots off, and for two months I never wore pyjamas. When I did take off my boots, they looked like they had been boiled in a washtub; they didn't look normal" (Leydesdorff 2011, p. 165).

The women of Srebrenica were one of the main drivers that led to Srebrenica being declared a safe zone. On March 12, 1993, General Philippe Morillon, the UN peacekeeping commander in Bosnia, set out on a fact-finding mission to check on reports of mass starvation in the enclave, without permission from his superiors, and visited the besieged enclave. Naser Orić, commander of Army of the Republic of Bosnia and Herzegovina (ARBiH) and the town's leaders wanted to prevent Morillon from leaving but to do it in a 'civilised way," (Rohde 2012, Page 45-46) as they were days away from being besieged by the Serb forces.

And so, Morillon's car and convoy was encircled by desperate women who protested him leaving, imploring him to save their lives. He tried to sneak out during the night, but was discovered and had to return, his actions being perceived as a humiliation to the UN (Rohde 2012, Page 45-46). This incident demonstrates one of the ways that the civilian women were actors in the events in Srebrenica, and that these stories are overlooked in the narratives told around Srebrenica.

The women were mobilised by Fatima Huseinović, president of the Women's League, who enabled "the women of Srebrenica to do their part in Srebrenica's fight for survival" (Honig and Both, 1996, p. 86). She went from house to house, assembled women, made signs and posters and arranged for his car to be blocked (Honig and Both, 1996, p. 86).

When Morillon attempts to leave the panicked women who fear for their lives and for those of their children, surround his car and chant in Bosnian "No! No!" "We want you; we want you!" (Fink 2003, p. 136) A young woman "knocks on the driver's side window of Morillon's car" and when it opens "she unleashes a gush of words. "It's a shame for the entire world!" she cries hoarsely in Bosnian and tells him they won't let him leave. She continues "I've been kept from my home for over a year.... Thank you, America, for the food.... Everybody here knows about the little food packages that's not enough. A year!" (Fink 2003, p. 136)

Behind her the women begin crying in a "sea of frustration" and so Morillon "pushes his way around the car and clambers backwards onto the hood, seeking high ground" to speak to the women (Fink 2003, p. 136). He attempts to convince them that he is not abandoning them "[t]he UNPROFOR soldiers will stay here" but the crowd counter asking about grenades and wail in frustration at the hardship they have endured for a year (Fink 2003, p. 136).

And so they wore him down with their protestations and pleas, and some "women lay in front of his vehicle" and Morillon "smoking one cigarette after the other" attempts negotiating "with the women for hours until he finally accepted that he had been taken hostage" (Honig and Both 1996, p. 86).

Rohde states that the "following day, when Morillon made his now famous declaration from the post office window—"You are now under the protection of the United Nations...I will never abandon you"—his aides burst out laughing. They knew Morillon did not have permission to make the desperate promise and he hand no way to keep it" (Rohde 2012, p. 45). While it was the Bosnian army who made the decision to keep Morillon on Srebrenica and exert pressure on him, it was the women who made this happen.

Women as the missing link

The plight of mothers and wives who were the missing link and became separated from their male offspring and husbands as the males trekked through the woods on foot to escape the clutches of the Serb forces who were set upon their extermination. The Serb forces were set upon a path of killing all males in the vicinity to ensure that no expelled Muslims could claim back Srebrenica. This exodus was called the Death March and the organisation Remembering Srebrenica report that an estimated that 15,000 entered the woods to escape and embarked on a five-day trek that covered 112 kilometres as they were hunted by the Serbs who coerced, tricked and let of poisonous gas to capture those escaping. Only 3,000 men survived the Death March with reporters describing "an army of ghosts" arriving at Tuzla (Remembering Srebrenica 2014).

These mothers and daughters and wives were the survivors who were the only ones left to provide testimony. Leydesdorff extensively interviewed female survivors about their loss and demonstrates how these moments of goodbye became frozen in time. She relates an interview by Timka who lost her husband and son and their farewell before they fled through the woods:

> Everything seemed to be in slow motion; one of the most painful moments; the grief she felt then took her breath away. Here again was the inevitable farewell, where one must pause. Timka regained her composure and continued: "I can't describe saying goodbye. My son's last words were, 'Mother, we are going now. Take care of the children.' Then they left, and I haven't hard from them since." She learned later that her husband, son, and son-in-law were all captured (Leydesdorff 2011, p. 14).

Leydesdorff (2011) relates numerous examples of these moments and delves further into this trauma of goodbye that the women suffer and how these do not seem to be their own memories "but rather they were like a film that was being played repeatedly. The trauma is not part of her life story; it has never been integrated" (p. 14)

She goes on to share a theory from a book about trauma, *The Haunted Self*, Onno van der Hart, Ellert Nijenhuis, and Kathy Steele who:

> note that the inability to give meaning to what has happened is characteristic of those who have suffered trauma. In order to get a grip on their lives again, victims need to attach meaning in various ways to what

> happened and to find a tentative explanation of why it happened. The events that led to the trauma must become reality, specifically a reality in the past and not one in which the events happened to another self, or were dream like or far removed. What happened must be accorded a place in one's life story and be available for conscious reflection. But it is extremely difficult to accept that something is part of you if it is draped over your consciousness like an inexplicable, black layer of fear (Leydesdorff 2011, p. 147).

Their goodbye symbolises these mothers who did not ever get a reunion and are forever frozen in time.

These female survivors also served another purpose which is that:

> They have literally been the embodiment of the search for and identification of the missing in more than one way. They have preserved a link between those who perished and those who survived, both through their narrated and documented memories of the missing men and though their bodies—their own DNA being a crucial piece of information required to establish identities of the missing (Halilovich 2014a, p. 240).

This demonstrates that the women are the links to the missing both in terms of holding and sharing their memories, which make up the recorded testimony, as well as the DNA link that has helped identify remains found in mass graves.

The Srebrenica Genocide Memorial, officially known as the Srebrenica–Potočari Memorial and Cemetery for the Victims of the 1995 Genocide, is the memorial-cemetery complex in Srebrenica set up to honour the victims of the 1995 Srebrenica massacre. The victims—at least 8,372 of them—were mainly male, mostly Muslim Bosniaks. To date, 94 mass gravesites have been exhumed in and around Srebrenica, and 6,900 victims have been positively identified. The search continues, however, for more than 1,700 victims who are still missing, (Memorial Center Srebrenica).

The first victims of genocide denial

The female survivors of Srebrenica embodied the loss of Srebrenica, because even as they lost their loved ones, they were trapped in a limbo without information or support from the international community or the Bosnian government. There were stories of miracles that they lived on with some Muslim men having "taken refuge in the forests near Srebrenica after the massacre" and straggling "across the front lines at night" to find their loved ones in Tuzla, living behind Serb lines, "sheltering in deserted Muslim villages" (Sudetic 1998, p. 332).

These women lived on borrowed hope, fuelled by would-be mystics and fortune tellers, like a *hodža* who "had gone to school to study the Koran but never finished the course" and found that "Allah blessed him with a mystical power" that "he discovered accidentally when he correctly prophesied that a woman from his village would give birth to a son" (Sudetic 1998, p. 333-334). So, he studied "with a dervish for eight years" who showed him "how to cure the sick and taught him the special prayers for exorcising demons and the art of locating missing people through numerology" (Sudetic 1998, p. 333-334).

Sudetic (1998) shared the story of Sanela, who turned to the hodža who correctly guessed identifying information about her missing husband and then told her to "to find a virgin girl who would volunteer to follow a ritual and attempt to dream about Muhamed" (p. 333-334). However, when she returned with the tale of the dream that he was unable to divine, Sanela then found an old mystic woman who had visions that told her he was "imprisoned in a labour camp surrounded by water" and that she would get word of him (Sudetic 1998, p. 333-334).

All throughout Tuzla, in the makeshift tent camps that the women survived in, they searched for word about their missing husbands and sons, until the "leaders of the Srebrenica women had organised and planned the memorial with the help of the American government" (Sudetic 1998, p. 343-344).

One year after the massacre, a memorial service and fundraising event was organised by the Queen Noor of Jordan and Swanee Hunt, the socialite U.S. ambassador to Austria, together with Fatima Huseinovic who was president of Women of Srebrenica, which "yielded a $5 million pledge in U.S. aid, plus $2.5 million from the European Union" (Simons 1996). Amra Begić Fazlić, Deputy Director of the Srebrenica Memorial Center, explained that it was their activism that "led to the establishment of the Memorial Center in 2000" (Arolsen Archives 2022).

These women "hadn't had an opportunity to read anything about Srebrenica in an entire year and didn't have televisions to watch. Bosnia's Muslim leaders, afraid they might be called to account for the military fiasco that led to the deaths of about eight thousand people had buried the issue" (Sudetic 1998, p. 343-344).

A large screen beamed a:

> special videotaped presentation" and the women saw "themselves huddled beside a fence near the decrepit

battery factory in Potočari on July 12, 1995. They were seeing themselves file down the asphalt road carrying their bags and bedding and climbing aboard buses. They were seeing themselves huddling around Mladić the man who had not even come out of hiding to attend the Serb memorial ceremony. Howls and screams sounded from the bleachers as if the devil himself had materialised from the chalky air (Sudetic 1998, p. 343-344).

Then they saw "pictures of Muslim men surrendering near Kravica pictures of men emerging from a forest, walking through waist-high grass down the hill behind the farmers' co-op" and "the arena erupted in cries of anguish" as women recognised their husbands, with some women fainting from the shock and horror (Sudetic 1998, p. 346).

Sudetic (1998) reports watching all this "standing on the basketball floor, taking all this down in my notebook, knowing full well that the State Department opposed an exhumation and identification of the remains in the three dozen mass graves around Srebrenica (p. 345). He stated that in the year since the massacre "hundreds of bodies rotted away in the meadows and woodlots and forests on the hillside above the farmers' co-op in Kravica" and that "[c]orpses lay strewn about the hilltop above the Konjević Poljo road" (Sudetic 1998, p. 346).

Even as they were fighting for the truth about their menfolk and helping to establish a memorial to share the truth of what happened, these women were battling squalor and hardship. Leydesdorff (2011) interviewed the women of Srebrenica in 2005 in a camp Mihatovići and found that "estimated that about 2,500 people who were originally from Srebrenica lived there" (p. 16-17). The camp was "a model of gloom and depression" as there was "chronic lack of maintenance" and "filth" and "stench and even "on a cold, snow-covered day in winter, the camp stinks" (Leydesdorff 2011, p. 16-17). There were "high levels of crime, which is the easiest way to acquire money" and residents "did not feel safe" however they were trapped and unable to return home to Srebrenica because many "houses were damaged or in ruins, the deeds had been lost, and there was no work to generate money for repairs and maintenance" (Leydesdorff 2011, p. 16-17). Furthermore, there was no way for these women to feel safe in Srebrenica as it was now needed to Republica Sprpska which meant that those in power "are the same ones who tried to murder you" (Leydesdorff 2011, p. 16-17).

Village women as the face of prejudice

One of the perspectives that is underplayed when looking at the Srebrenica massacre is that of the prejudice toward Muslim women by the Dutch peacekeepers, and the fact that these were the women that were most victimised by the Serbs.

To the Dutch the Muslim population were one people turning on each other, however, during the three years of siege as the Serbs tightened the noose around Srebrenica and waged a campaign of terror through starvation, shelling and snipers, the population internally seethed with tension between the urban and rural populations fighting for resources.

Jan William Honig and Norbert Both (1996) confirm that "Dutch contact with the Bosnian Muslim population remained limited" (p. 131). The Dutch soldiers found the sight of the starving refugees a confronting spectacle with their hygiene issues that led to skin diseases and other illnesses and:

> reported being struck by the massive numbers of
> Muslims who 'wandered around aimlessly.' Some
> Dutch were shocked by the eagerness with which
> Muslims await the dumping of rubbish on the tip
> outside the compound in order to scan it for us-
> able items or food. Burglary in the compounds and
> OPs [observation posts] was a constant menace. Many
> soldiers spoke in disparaging terms of the Muslims
> (Honig and Both 1996, p.131).

As a former resident of Srebrenica, Hasan Hasanović (2016) confirms this when in his memoir *Surviving Srebrenica* and states "I always had the impression that they looked at us as miserable and disgusting people, but of course not all Dutch soldiers looked at us that way" (p. 48).

The peacekeepers were racist towards the Muslim population, and this was due to Islamophobia. When we look at the Yugoslav population, we need to understand that Serbs, Croats and Bosnians were racially identical because it highlights the fact that the discrimination and ethnic cleansing that was committed against the inhabitants of Srebrenica was based on religion. It is also important because it underscores that fact that it was impossible to differentiate physically the various nationalities in the conflict. This differentiation could only be accomplished by "profiling" which involves the reading of visual cues or assumptions based on physical appearance, clothing, and other external markers to determine if someone was Bosnian, Serb, or Croat. This "profiling" plays a part in the interactions between Dutch peacekeepers and the Bosniak population.

To the Dutch peacekeepers, the Muslim women from villages presented a confronting sight. Many of those who were cleansed and poured into Srebrenica came from villages that dotted the mountains of eastern Srebrenica. Fink states that many of these villages were made of residents who all shared the same surname as their descendants "had settled there and multiplied and one day the family grew as numerous as a village" (Fink 2003, p. 38).

Tea Hadžiristić (2017) observes that in the 1800s "habits of veiling or head-covering were present among all religious groups" including Orthodox, Catholic, Muslim, and Sephardic Jewish, and over the years the fashions with women covering themselves changed and describes how in the mid-19th century wealthy women returning from Turkey adopted the "zar, a burqa-like garment which covered the whole body and face" which quickly became fashionable among Muslim women (Hadžiristić 2017, p. 184). During the Austrian occupation the Muslim community felt threatened in "becoming a religious minority in a Catholic empire" and thus "began to retreat into the Islamic community" and as "Muslim women adopted the zar on a mass scale" they were then "excluded from schooling, and lost the privileged status they had enjoyed in the Ottoman Empire" (Hadžiristić 2017, p.184).

Eventually veiling became a marker of identity of the Bosnian Muslims and:

> Islam became the sole carrier of all that was oppressive about the patriarchal system. In this process, all of the negative traits that the local community presumed to be associated with veiling—patriarchal family relations, female illiteracy, lack of political consciousness, female unemployment, old-fashioned gender norms, violence against women, and seclusion in the home —were handed over onto the Muslim population,

even though they could be found in the Christian population as well (Hadžiristić 2017 p. 187).

In this way we can there was a change within Yugoslav society and Huisman and Hondagneu-Sotelo (2005) contend that "Western European form of dress was adopted widely in urban areas, but less fervently in rural areas" (p. 49). Furthermore, that as industrialisation demanded women enter the workforce, "veils were outlawed, but headscarves were legally permitted" (Huisman and Hondagneu-Sotelo 2005, p. 54).

Women wore headscarves and billowy pants, or *šamije*, and *dimije*. This is a schism that is played out in the differences in clothing between urban and rural areas. Urban areas tended to adopt more modern and Western styles, while rural areas maintained traditional clothing that more closely reflected their social and religious beliefs.

This indicates that the attitudes in Srebrenica toward the women who wore *dimije* and headscarfs represent the battle between the forward-thinking Western attitudes that flourished during communism and the view that those who adhered to religious modesty were backwards in their thinking. The cultural aspect of the division between the urban and rural residents in Srebrenica, with women wearing *dimije* when they were in their homes in the village and then choosing not to wear them in the more urban Srebrenica as this would have marked them as refugees thus showcasing the ongoing tension between urban and traditional practices.

Electricity and plumbing had only been introduced in these villages within the past two decades prior to the war, with women having to walk to wells to fetch water prior to that. The villagers were self-sufficient subsisting on the vegetables they grew, the sheep or cows they raised, and the women would spin wool and knit clothes. A high proportion were illiterate schooling came second to household chores and children were kept at home to work on household chores (Fink 2003, p. 38).

The women from the villages wore headscarves, *šamije*, and *dimije*, billowy harem pants, and aged prematurely from the hard physical labour of their village lives. They did not have access to dental care, and many suffered extreme gum disease and teeth loss.

This prejudice was exemplified by a cartoon left on the barrack wall of the Potočari compound by the peacekeepers that reads:

"*No teeth.*

Has moustache.

Smells like shit.

Bosnian Girl" (Kamerić, Š (n.d.) *Bosnian Girl Series)*.

The Dutch military authorities instructed male UN peacekeepers regarding their interactions with Muslim women "to avoid eye contact [...], not to speak openly with them [...], nor shake hands with them" (NIOD, Part II: 226). These instructions came from a poor understanding of the Islamic practices of Bosniak people" (Rozman-Clark 2014).

This illustrates that rural women were subjected to prejudice both by the Bosniak urban population, and the peacekeepers, and during the three days that the Bosniak population was terrorised by Chetniks at Potočari, it was the Bosniak rural women who were targeted by sexual violence.

One of the contested areas in representing the fall is the culpability of the Dutch peacekeepers, and the perception by the Bosniak population that they were betrayed by the UN.

Leydesdorff reports from the testimony of the women who survived that when the enclave fell, DutchBat soldiers urged people to go to Potočari, giving the impression they would be safe there. This directive, however, played into the hands of the Serb forces. Survivors recount that from several villages, the route to the UN compound was not straightforward, and yet, an endless stream of people walked to Potočari, driven by the belief that the UN base would provide safety. They were tragically mistaken (Leydesdorff 2011, p. 151). Many were killed on the road to Potočari, either from the crush of people or by direct violence, and then the men and boys were transported to be massacred and buried in mass graves.

During the fall of Srebrenica, when 30,000 residents sought refuge in Potočari, DutchBat soldiers faced the overwhelming task of protecting the population without air support and while being outnumbered. Survivor accounts, such as those documented by Leydesdorff, reveal a disturbing picture. While some soldiers feared for their lives, others displayed a shocking level of insensitivity: "I do blame them for dancing and singing, that they celebrated on the occasion of our tragedy. They weren't on our side; they partied with the Serbs. As human beings, they shouldn't have done that" (Leydesdorff 2011, p. 156).

The reality that the peacekeepers on the ground did expect air strikes to be deployed by the UN, however this did not eventuate, leaving both the peacekeepers as the Bosniak population at the mercy of the Serb soldiers.

The Bosniak population saw the UN as Serb puppets because they were using Dutch peacekeepers as hostages to prevent NATO from actioning airstrikes that would save the enclave from the Serb onslaught. Rohde (2012) brings this to life through an anecdote shared by Dutch peacekeeper Egbers who was stopped by a Bosnian farmer who through sign language indicated that:

> There would be no NATO air strikes because of the Dutch hostages. UN commanders or the Dutch government would hold back, fearing the Serbs would kill Dutch hostages in retaliation. The lives of thirty Dutch soldiers were worth more than the lives of 30,000 Muslims. Egbers stared at the ground and suddenly felt very uncomfortable. It won't come to that, he thought. They can save all of us (pp. 68-69).

The bias of peacekeepers against the Bosniak population also played a part in the fall of the enclave. When Karremans, the former commander of Dutchbat troops in Srebrenica, was seeking air strikes he did not include an incident of a hand grenade that "had blown the Dutch APC off the road near Camila Omanovic house at 7: 15 am" as he believed that this was done by the Muslims (Rohde 2012, page 102).

Rohde (2012) confirms that this disconnect is based on fact with Karremans, the Dutch commander of Dutchbat troops in Srebrenica informing:

> the officers in Srebrenica that massive air strikes would be launched against the Serbs the following day if they did not withdraw from the enclave. But the actual warning—which was also faxed to Karremans—stated only that the UN 'demands' that the Bosnian Serbs withdraw from the enclave. There was no mention of massive air strikes if the Serbs failed to withdraw. ... The disarray in the nearly all-Dutch command chain was as tragic as it was inexcusable (p. 88).

In one sense, both the peacekeepers and the Bosniaks were the victims of the conflict: the peacekeepers in not being equipped or supported by the UN and the Bosniaks not being protected by the UN. The whole UN mission of keeping the Srebrenica enclave a safe zone was a tragic failure from the beginning, because it was declared a safe zone under duress when the starvation of its civilians was publicised. And the failure was punctuated by its tragic conclusion when Srebrenica fell and the UN did not use air strikes to protect the population and deter the Serb attack, thus preventing the very predictable massacre.

Rape as ethnic cleansing

Rape was a tool used to terrorise and ethnically cleanse the Muslim territories due to the particular brand of patriarchy that enabled this within the Balkans. The use of rape highlights ongoing social and political issues of patriarchy, as Serbs used rape as a form of ethnic cleaning, and the Muslim community sidelined these victims in memorials and history due to the notions of shame and patriarchy within their communities.

First, there is the need to understand the role of females under the Balkan patriarchal system. For centuries within Yugoslav identity the "extended family represented the core of the patriarchal lineage" under which "material goods were communally held by the patrilineage" which was called a *zadruga* (Olujic as cited in Snyder, Gabbard, May, and Zulcic 2006, pp. 187-188). Within this system women moved into her husband's house and lived "under their authority" (Cockburn as cited in Snyder, Gabbard, May, and Zulcic 2006, pp. 187-188) and "were primarily valued as wives and mothers" and "symbolised the family's code of honour/shame, as evident in the highly controlled aspects of their chastity, marital virtue, and fertility" (Olujic as cited in Snyder, Gabbard, May, and Zulcic 2006, pp. 187-188).

While the *zadruga* prevailed until the 1970s this "ideology still remains at the core of Yugoslavian cultural identity" (Olujic as cited in Snyder, Gabbard, May, and Zulcic 2006, pp. 187-188) and women continue to be subordinated to patriarchal culture and "lacked equality with men in inheritance, property rights, and family laws" (Bozinovic as cited in Snyder, Gabbard, May, and Zulcic 2006, pp. 187-188). They were also excluded from positions of executive leadership and political authority because of "the lack of day care facilities" and so still were "socially defined by, the domestic responsibilities of their house-holds" with domestic violence being common (Cockburn as cited in Snyder, Gabbard, May, and Zulcic 2006, pp. 187-188).

The role of Muslim honour was used against the Bosniak population and that this is why rape was deployed as a weapon, as demonstrated in testimony from Alexandra Stiglmayer book *Mass Rape: The War Against Women in Bosnia-Herzegovina* "[w]e saw them rape the *hadji's* daughter—one after the other, they raped her. The *hadji* had to watch too. When they were done, they rammed a knife into his throat" (Khan 2019, p. 237).

A *hadji* is a Muslim person who completes the pilgrimage to Mecca, which is one of the five pillars of Islam, and as such, they are given the title as a sign of respect and honour. Through this passage we see that the *hadji's* daughter was singled out for rape so that Serbs are symbolically also defiling the Islam.

"A report by the World Council of Churches (WCC) maintained that the use of rape as a weapon of war is perceived as having its roots in patriarchal systems" because the "destruction and violation of women" is a way of attacking the male opponents as they cannot protect their women (Salzman 1998, p. 365). Olujic (1998) states that "war rape would not work as well as a policy of terror were it not for the cultural salience within the honour/shame complex generalised in the southeastern European cultural area" because in this culture "female chastity is central to family and community honour" (as cited in Snyder, Gabbard, May, and Zulcic, 2006, p. 190). As such, they are "dishonouring a woman's body" and symbolically dishonouring the whole lineage (Snyder, Gabbard, May, and Zulcic 2006, p. 190).

However, there was also another darker, more diabolical reason at play. Muslim women who were raped also had to contend with the notion of a "violation of a woman's honour" (Salzman 1998, p. 367) which is not only about her own personal morality, but her family's and community's reputation. Rape "produces various, often contradictory, religious and cultural responses" (Salzman 1998, p. 367) because in traditional and patriarchal societies, and in some interpretations of Islamic culture, this notion of a woman's honour is tied to sexual purity. Even though when a woman is raped, it is not her fault, her honour can still be seen as tainted (Salzman 1998, p. 367).

Salzman (1998) argues that the "Serbian governmental and military powers appear to have utilised systematic rape as a weapon of war to serve their overall objective of 'ethnic cleansing'" (p. 354). While rape occurred "against the women on all sides of the conflict in Bosnia: Serbs, Croats, and Muslims" what differentiated the Serbian practice of rape and sexual assault against Muslims on Serbian territory was what the United Nations Commission of Experts concluded that "the practices of 'ethnic cleansing,' sexual assault and rape have been carried out by some of the parties so systematically that they strongly appear to be the product of a policy" (Salzman 1998, pp. 355-356). Rape helped to "eradicate the enemy" by dispersing "them through forced migration" (Snyder, Gabbard, May, and Zulcic, 2006, p. 191). As a result, approximately 5 million Yugoslavians, most of whom were women and children, were displaced (Snyder, Gabbard, May, and Zulcic 2006, p. 191).

The Yugoslav National Army UNA Psychological Operations Department in Belgrade developed a strategic military and political plan to drive Muslims out of Bosnia based on an analysis of Muslim behaviour which "showed that their morale, desire for battle, and will could be crushed more easily by raping women, especially minors and even children, and by killing members of the Muslim nationality inside their religious facilities" (Salzman 1998, p. 356).

MacDonald alludes to how Islamophobia, or a fear of "Eastern customs and manners" inspired disinformation and propaganda designed to incite fear and hatred (MacDonald 2003, p. 235-236). They spread a false narrative that stated that Islamic fundamentalists from Sarajevo were singling out healthy Serbian women out for "special treatment" where they are "impregnated by orthodox Islamic seed in order to raise a generation of janissaries on the territories they surely consider to be theirs, the Islamic republic" (MacDonald 2003, p. 235-236).

Using the word "janissaries" taps into deep-seated historical memories of Ottoman rule over the Balkans when Christian boys were forcibly taken, converted into Islam and trained as soldiers for the empire (Malcolm 1994, p. 46). So through this imagery, they imply that these actions are part of a plan to create a new generation of Muslims reminiscent of how the Ottomans created Janissaries.

However, in this passage, the focus is on the imagery of Serb women being impregnated by "orthodox Islamic seed" (MacDonald 2003, p. 235-236), framing Muslims as invaders seeking to biologically alter the population through sexual violence. This echoes xenophobic tropes about the "other" being a threat to women, culture, and race, and plays on the fear of religious and racial contamination, suggesting that the very lineage of Serbs is under attack. Through this, the propaganda is reviving a historical grievance to deepen ethnic divides and inflame nationalist fervour. MacDonald goes on to state that this propaganda was used to deflect "criticism of any Serbian-inspired rape policy" (MacDonald 2003, pp. 235-236). This is confirmed by Gutman (1993a), who reports on a gang rape by Bosniak victim and the soldier tells her "That's what your people are doing to us as well" (p. 66).

There was a psychological aspect of using rape as a tool of genocide that was particularly influenced by Balkan patriarchal society where "the family name passes on through the male, regardless of religion or ethnicity" (Salzman 1998, pp. 364-365). The cultural and genetic myth that this is based on is "that a child born from rape by a Serb will always be considered Serbian" (Salzman 1998, pp. 364-365). While the rape itself is about inciting terror, it is also about using rape to corrupt and dilute the Muslim bloodlines and commit a form of cultural or genetic extermination by erasing or tainting the group's future generations. The acceptance of the myth is dependant not just on the perpetrators "buying into the genetic and cultural myth" but the "victims, their families, and their communities" (Salzman 1998, pp. 364-365). Catholic and Muslim women who referred to their foetuses a "filth" or "that thing" internalised this myth of contamination and through their dehumanising language" (Salzman 1998, pp. 364-365) and demonstrated their psychological trauma that they have been defiled, and they cannot emotionally or culturally connect with the pregnancy as it is a product of violence and destruction.

The term ethnic cleansing was used to hide the real intent, which was genocide and, as such, rape was used as a way of ethnically cleansing Bosniak Muslims from Serb territories. This particular type of violence and horror could only flourish within this particularly patriarchal society, whereby honour was tied to women's chastity and purity. This theory was inspired by Islamophobia and the othering of Muslims and using propaganda to cast this as vengeance against Muslim perpetrators who were supposedly raping Serb women to justify the retaliation.

This demonstrates that the role of rape within this war highlights the ongoing social and political role of patriarchy within the Balkans and within Muslim communities that has led to these women being disempowered and silenced.

The experiences and roles of women within the context of the Srebrenica genocide illuminate the profound resilience and courage they displayed in the face of unimaginable suffering. From their pivotal role in preventing General Morillon from leaving Srebrenica and securing its designation as a "safe zone," to their relentless activism in establishing the Srebrenica Memorial Center, women shaped both the course of history and its enduring remembrance. They preserved the bond between survivors and the deceased through DNA identification and testimonies, ensuring that the truth of what happened would not be erased. Their defiance of genocide denial, even when the international community and Bosnian government initially failed to exhume the bodies, underscores their determination to preserve memory and seek justice.

However, their experiences also reflect the compounded layers of victimhood, as they bore the brunt of ethnic cleansing, with rape being wielded as a tool to weaponise cultural notions of honour against the Bosniak population. The women of Srebrenica became symbols of prejudice, suffering abuse not only from Serb forces but also neglect from Dutch peacekeepers. These portrayals reveal the duality of their role: as victims of systemic violence and as agents of resistance and healing. By examining their experiences, we gain critical insight into the broader narrative of the Bosnian War, understanding the gendered dimensions of conflict, the mechanisms of genocide denial, and the enduring fight for justice and commemoration.

Conclusion

Fiction has a role in shaping the public understanding of genocide, justice and memory, especially in light of historical denial and political revisionism. As such literature has a role in performing an ethical intervention by challenging harmful narratives, correcting historical distortions, and giving voice to those who have been silenced or marginalised—especially in contexts of violence, oppression, or injustice.

Future studies might expand this inquiry by analysing how Bosnian authors themselves reconstruct memory, or how these novels are received in educational and public settings. This research reveals the necessity for authors to interrogate the myths and inaccuracies surrounding the Bosnian War, particularly those perpetuated by dominant Western narratives. There is an urgent need to critically examine the rural-urban divide within Bosnia, a division that deeply shaped community identities and ultimately influenced the dynamics leading up to the Srebrenica genocide. By addressing these oversights, literature can resist historical erasure and serve as a vehicle for both remembrance and education, especially in a world where truth and history are increasingly contested.

There is also scope to investigate the pedagogical role of fiction in teaching genocide studies or preventing historical erasure. Currently the Australian curriculum has introduced a compulsory year 10 subject titled *The Modern World and Australia* and within this subject description is the World War II (1939-45) which is to investigate wartime experiences through a study of World War II in depth, including the Holocaust and use of the atomic bomb (ACDSEH107) (Australian Curriculum, Assessment and Reporting Authority [ACARA], n.d.). Within the Victorian Curriculum Holocaust Education –Delivery Requirements is the guidance to "focus on the people of the Holocaust—victims/survivors, the righteous, the perpetrators, collaborators and bystanders" and to "avoid comparing the 'severity' of the Holocaust to other genocides, and comparing suffering" (Department of Education and Training Victoria, n.d.).

I believe that this should be extended into further genocide studies that focus on the concept of dehumanisation, instead of using the "two distinct terms: antisemitism and Islamophobia" (Hashemi 2024). Dehumanisation "involves seeing certain groups as inhuman or subhuman, so undeserving of equal treatment" (Hashemi 2024). By broadening the scope of genocide studies to look at the concept of dehumanisation it gives students the opportunity to see and understand the role of 'othering' and 'discrimination' and its role in conflict, and within contemporary 'everyday' society.

In a world where historical truth is increasingly contested, fiction does not merely reflect memory—it shapes it. And in the case of Srebrenica, that shaping is not just literary—it is moral, cultural, and deeply political. Thus, there is an urgency and responsibility in educating people about the factors that lead these rifts in society, and the role of literature in shaping cultural memory—what Pierre Nora refers to as *lieuxde mémoire*, or sites of memory—where the past is preserved and interpreted in the absence of continuous lived experience.

Historical novels, especially those dealing with genocide, do not simply reflect history; they construct frameworks through which readers come to understand and emotionally engage with it. As such, they carry immense ethical and cultural responsibility. This work demonstrates that fiction, when responsibly crafted, can contribute meaningfully to cultural understanding, historical justice, and the ongoing memorialisation of trauma.

Handout: Organisations and Resources to Learn More About Srebrenica

The Srebrenica genocide stands as a pivotal moment in modern history, serving as both a reminder of the consequences of hatred and an enduring call for justice and reconciliation. Below is a curated list of organisations and resources for readers interested in exploring the history, memory, and ongoing impact of Srebrenica.

Key Organisations

Srebrenica Memorial Center https://srebrenicamemorial.org/

Remembering Srebrenica https://www.srebrenica.org.uk/

Arolsen Archives https://arolsen-archives.org/en/news/remembering-srebrenica/

Institute for Research of Genocide Canada (IGC) http://instituteforgenocide.org/

International Commission on Missing Persons (ICMP) https://www.icmp.int/

Educational Resources

United Nations International Residual Mechanism for Criminal Tribunals (IRMCT) https://www.irmct.org/

Genocide Studies and Prevention Journal https://scholarcommons.usf.edu/gsp/

Facing History and Ourselves https://www.facinghistory.org/

Books

Postcards from the Grave by Emir Suljagić

Endgame: The Betrayal and Fall of Srebrenica by David Rohde

War Hospital: A True Story of Surgery and Survival by Sheri Fink

A Witness to Genocide: The First Inside Account of the Horrors of 'Ethnic Cleansing' in Bosnia by Roy Gutman

Surviving Srebrenica by Hasan Hasanovic

Surviving the Bosnian Genocide: The Women of Srebrenica Speak by Selma Leydesdorff

The Bridge Betrayed: Religion and Genocide in Bosnia by Michael A. Sells

Blood and Vengeance: One Family's Story of the War in Bosnia by Chuck Sudetic

Srebrenica: Record of a War Crime by Jan Willem Honig and Norbert Both

The War is Dead, Long Live the War: Bosnia: The Reckoning by Ed Vulliamy

Documentaries and Films

Quo Vadis, Aida? (2020)

Srebrenica: A Cry from the Grave (1999)

Miss Sarajevo (1997)

Online Archives and Digital Tools

Srebrenica Genocide Blog http://srebrenica-genocide.blogspot.com/

Yad Vashem's Genocide Studies Resources https://www.yadvashem.org/

Get Involved

- Attend a local *Remembering Srebrenica* event or webinar.

- Support organisations like the Srebrenica Memorial Center through donations or volunteering.

- Share stories and resources to raise awareness about the Srebrenica genocide and its ongoing lessons for humanity.

By exploring these organisations and resources, readers can deepen their understanding of Srebrenica's history and contribute to the global effort to ensure that such atrocities are never repeated.

Bibliography

Ali, Rabia., and Lifschultz, Lawrence. 1994. "Why Bosnia?" *Third World Quarterly*, 15 (3), pp. 367–401. https://doi.org/10.1080/01436599408420387

Arolsen Archives. (2022). "Remembering Srebrenica" *Arolsen Archives*. [online] https://arolsen-archives.org/en/news/remembering-srebrenica/ [Accessed 19 January 2025].

Australian Curriculum, Assessment and Reporting Authority. (n.d.). *History: Year 9 – The environment movement and development of environmental policies, including the influence of climate change* [ACDSEH128]. Australian Curriculum.

Botev, Nikolai. 1994. "Where East Meets West: Ethnic Intermarriage in the Former Yugoslavia, 1962 to 1989". *American Sociological Review*, 59 (3), pp. 461–480. https://doi.org/10.2307/2095944

Bringa, Tone. 2002. "Averted gaze: Genocide in Bosnia-Herzegovina, 1992-1995." Edited by Alexander Laban Hinton, *Annihilating difference: The anthropology of genocide* (pp. 194-225). University of California Press.

De Groot, Jerome. 2009. *The Historical Novel*. London: Routledge.

Department of Education and Training Victoria. n.d.. *Characteristics of Holocaust educa-*

tion. https://www2.education.vic.gov.au/pal/holocaust-education-delivery-requirements/guidance/characteristics-holocaust-education

Fink, Sheri. 2003. *War Hospital: A True Story of Surgery and Survival*. Public Affairs.

Gutman, Roy. 1993a. *A Witness to Genocide: The First Inside Account of the Horrors of "Ethnic Cleansing" in Bosnia*. Macmillan.

Gutman, Roy. 1993b. "U.N. Forces Accused of Using Serb-Run Brothel." *The Washington Post*. 1 November 1993. https://www.washingtonpost.com/archive/politics/1993/11/02/un-forces-accused-of-using-serb-run-brothel/78414de2-36d0-41c0-9081-c3a5ee513078/ [Accessed 24 September 2024].

Hadžiristić, Tea. 2017. "Unveiling Muslim Women in Socialist Yugoslavia: the Body between Socialism, Secularism, and Colonialism." *Religion and Gender (Utrecht)*, *7* (2), pp. 184–203. https://doi.org/10.18352/rg.10137

Hasanovic, Hasan. 2016. *Surviving Srebrenica*. Aberdeenshire: Lumphanan Press.

Halilovich, Hariz. 2016. "Re-imaging and re-imagining the past after 'memoricide': Intimate archives as inscribed memories of the missing." *Archival Science*, 16(1), pp. 77–92. https://doi.org/10.1007/s10502-015-9258-0

Honig, Jan Willem and Both, Norbert. 1996. *Srebrenica: Record of a War Crime*. London: Penguin Books.

Huisman, Kimberley., and Hondagneu-Sotelo, Pierrette. 2005. "Dress Matters: Change and Continuity in the Dress Practices of Bosnian Muslim Refugee Women." *Gender & Society*, *19* (1),pp. 44–65. https://doi.org/10.1177/0891243204269716

Iner, Dener 2024. "What is dehumanisation? Some want it to replace definitions of antisemitism and Islamophobia." *The Conversation*. 10 April 2025.

https://theconversation.com/what-is-dehumanisation-some-want-it-to-replace-definitions-of-antisemitism-and-islamophobia-253346[Accessed 10 April 2025].

International Criminal Tribunal for the Former Yugoslavia (ICTY). 2001. *Prosecutor v. Kunarac, Kovac and Vukovic* (IT-96-23-T & IT-96-23/1-T), Trial Chamber Judgment, 22 February 2001. https://www.icty.org/x/cases/kunarac/tjug/en/kun-tj010222e.pdf [Accessed 24 September 2024].

Kamerić, Šejla. *Bosnian Girl (Series)*. n.d. 6 screenprints on canvas in 6 color variations, 140 x 100 cm (55.1 x 39.4 in) each. fineartmultiple.com. Switzerland. https://fineartmultiple.com/sejla-kameric-bosnian-girl-series/?___store=en/ [Accessed 16 January 2024].

Karčić, Hikmet, and Newell, Richard. 2023. "The Bosnian Genocide as the Cornerstone for Bosnian Studies." In *Bosnian Studies*, edited by Dženata Karabegović and Adna Karamehić-Oates, pp. 19–46. Columbia: University of Missouri Press.

Karamehić-Oates, Adna. 2023. "Introduction" ." In *Bosnian Studies*, edited by Dženata Karabegović and Adna Karamehić-Oates, pp. 3–18. Columbia: University of Missouri Press.

Kukić, Leonard. 2023. "The Last Yugoslavs: Ethnic Diversity and National Identity", *Explorations in Economic History*, Volume 88, 2023, 101504, ISSN 0014-4983, https://doi.org/10.1016/j.eeh.2022.101504

Leydesdorff, Selma. 2015. *Surviving the Bosnian Genocide: The Women of Srebrenica Speak*. Indiana University Press.

Lendák-Kabók, Karolina. 2024. Mixedness in Conflict: The Impact of Yugoslav Wars on Intermarriages in the Western Balkans. *Sociology Compass*, 18(7). doi: https://doi.org/10.1111/soc4.13242

Malcolm, Noel. 1994. *Bosnia: A Short History*. London: Macmillan.

MacDonald, David Bruce. 2003. *Balkan Holocausts?: Serbian and Croatian victim-centred propaganda and the war in Yugoslavia*. Manchester University Press.

Mangafić, Jasmina, and Veselinović, Ljiljan. 2020. "The determinants of corruption at the individual level: Evidence from Bosnia-Herzegovina". *Economic Research-Ekonomska Istraživanja*, 33(1), pp. 2670–2691. https://doi.org/10.1080/1331677X.2020.17 23426

Memorial Center Srebrenica. n.d.. *Mass graves*. https://srebre nicamemorial.org/en/page/mass-graves/27 [Accessed 24 September 2024].

McCullagh, C. Behan. 1987. The Truth of Historical Narratives. *History and Theory: Studies in the Philosophy of History*, 26 (4), pp. 30–46. https://doi.org/10.2307/2505043

Meirison, Meirison. 2020. "Islamic tolerance on religious freedom, culture and thought in Andalusia." *Hikmatuna: Journal for Integrative Islamic Studies*, 6 (1), pp. 16-28. https://garuda.kemdikbud.go. id/documents/detail/3485792

Nora, Pierre. 1989. "Between Memory and History: Les Lieux de Mémoire." *Representations (Berkeley, Calif.)*, 26 (26), pp. 7–24. htt ps://doi.org/10.2307/2928520

Nuhanovic, Hasan. 2019. *The Last Refuge: A True Story of War, Survival and Life Under Siege in Srebrenica* (M. Evtov & A. Sluiter, Trans.). London: Peter Owen Publishers.

Palmberger, Monika. 2016. *How Generations Remember: Conflicting histories and shared memories in post-war Bosnia and Herzegovina*. London: Palgrave Macmillan.

Pajalic, Amra. 2023. "I was told to marry into my own faith. My daughter will get to choose." *The Age*. 5 April 2023. https://www.theage.com.au/lifestyle/life-and-relationships/i-was-tol

d-to-marry-into-my-own-faith-my-daughter-will-get-to-choose-2023 0404-p5cy2v.html

Prosecutor v. Kunarac, Case No. IT-96-23-T & IT-96-23/1-T, Trial Chamber Judgment, International Criminal Tribunal for the former Yugoslavia, 22 February 2001. https://www.icty.org/x/cases/kunarac/tjug/en/kun-tj010222e.pdf

Prosecutor v. Krstić, Case No. IT-98-33-A, Appeals Chamber Judgment (Int'l Crim. Trib. for the Former Yugoslavia. 19 April 2004. https://www.icty.org/x/cases/krstic/acjug/en/krs-aj040419e.pdf

Remembering Srebrenica. 2014. "The Death March." 24 June 2014. https://srebrenica.org.uk/what-happened/history/column. [Accessed 19 January 2025]

Rohde, David. 2012. *Endgame: The betrayal and fall of Srebrenica, Europe's worst massacre since World War II*. Penguin Books.

Rozman–Clark, Tea. 2014. *The United Nations Peacekeepers and Local Population of the United Nations Safe Area Srebrenica: (De) Construction of Human Relationships*, University of Nova Gorica Graduate School, Nova Gorica

Sacco, Joe. 2018. *Safe Area Goražde* s/c. Fantagraphics Books.

Salzman, Todd, A. 1998. "Rape camps as a means of ethnic cleansing: Religious, cultural, and ethical responses to rape victims in the former Yugoslavia." *Human Rights Quarterly*, 20(2), pp. 348–378. https://doi.org/10.1353/hrq.1998.0019

Sabic-El-Rayess, Amra. 2023. "Storytelling as a Method for Transformative Learning, Healing, Recognition, Inclusion and Empowerement." In *Bosnian Studies*, edited by Dženata Karabegović and Adna Karamehić-Oates, pp. 123-148. University of Missouri Press.

Sells, Michael, A. 1996. *The Bridge Betrayed: Religion and Genocide in Bosnia*. University of California Press.

Simic, Olivera. 2014. *Surviving Peace: A Political Memoir*. Spinifex Press.

Simons, Marlise. 1996. "Unforgiving." *Chicago Tribune*. 18 August 1996 Available at: https://www.chicagotribune.com/1996/08/18/unforgiving-2/ [Accessed 19 January 2025].

Sluga, Glenda. 2001. "Bodies, Souls and Sovereignty: The Austro-Hungarian Empire and the Legitimacy of Nations." *Ethnicities*, *1*(2), pp. 207–232. https://doi.org/10.1177/146879680100100203

Snyder, Cindy S., Gabbard, Wesley J., May, Jean D., & Zulcic, Nehada. 2006. "On the battle ground of women's bodies: Mass rape in Bosnia-Herzegovina." *Affilia*, 21(2), pp. 184–195. https://doi.org/10.1177/0886109905286017

Smits Jorean. 2010 "Ethnic Intermarriage and Social Cohesion. What Can We Learn from Yugoslavia?" *Soc Indic Res.* 28 May 2009, (3), pp. 417-432. https://pmc.ncbi.nlm.nih.gov/articles/PMC2848333/

Sudetic, Chuck. (1998). *Blood and vengeance: One family's story of the war in Bosnia*. W. W. Norton & Co Inc.

Suljagic, Emir. 2005. *Postcards from the Grave*. Saqi Books.

Tomić-Koludrović, Inga. and Petrić, Mirko. 2014 *Class in Yugoslav Socialism and in the Post-Yugoslav Societies: Toward a Bourdieuan Repositioning of the Issue* (Part 1), Institute of Social Sciences Ivo Pilar – Regional Centre Split, Croatia , Department of Sociology, University of Zadar, Croatia

United Nations International Criminal Tribunal for the Former Yugoslavia (ICTY). 2017. *Minka Čehajić. Voices of Victims Impact Statement*. https://www.icty.org/sid/186 [Accessed 23 September 2024].

United Nations Security Council. 2024. *Resolution 819: International Day of Reflection and Commemoration of the 1995 Genocide in*

Srebrenica (S/RES/819). https://documents.un.org/doc/undoc/ltd/n24/140/80/pdf/n2414080.pdf

United Nations International Criminal Tribunal for the Former Yugoslavia (ICTY). 2017. *Dr. Idriz Merdžanić. Voices of Victims Impact Statement*. https://www.icty.org/en/content/dr-idriz-merd%C5%BEani%C4%87 [Accessed 23 September 2024].

Vervaet, Stijn. 2011.*Writing war, writing memory. The representation of the recent past and the construction of cultural memory in contemporary Bosnian prose. Neohelicon (Budapest)*, *38* (1), pp. 1–17. https://doi.org/10.1007/s11059-010-0076-3

Vulliamy, Ed. 2005. "After the Massacre, a Homecoming." *The Guardian*, 30 April 2005. https://www.theguardian.com/lifeandstyle/2005/apr/30/weekend.edvulliamy [Accessed 3 November 2024].

Zilic, Ahmed. 1998. "Religious pluralism in Bosnia: Five centuries of convivencia, five years of conflict." *European Judaism*, 31 (1), pp. 15–25. https://www.jstor.org/stable/43740571

Glossary

Alija Izetbegović The Bosnian President. The Serbs used the name "Alija" as a derogatory slur for Bosnians.

Ašikovanje A traditional Bosnian dating ritual, often involving flirtatious conversation.

Austro-Hungarian empire Annexed Bosnia in 1879.

Babo Father.

Balija (plural Balije) A derogatory term used by Serbs for Bosniaks (Muslim South Slavs). The term is of Turkish origin and was originally applied to primitive Muslims or Muslim peasants.

Boiler The term given to improvised bombs dropped by Serbs from modified planes.

Bosniak A Muslim South Slav, primarily inhabiting Bosnia and Herzegovina. The term refers to an ethnic and cultural designation for a predominantly Muslim population in Bosnia and Herzegovina.

Bosnian A citizen of Bosnia and Herzegovina.

Bosnian Genocide Studies Explores the genocide through "the continued study of its roots, preparation, execution, and lingering aftermath".

Chetniks Serb paramilitary groups. They were originally a loose alliance of Serb nationalists and royalists during WWII who sought the establishment of a Greater Serbia cleansed of non-Serbs.

Dimije Harem pants worn by women in the Middle East.

Dido Grandfather.

Drina A river in Bosnia that runs through Serbia.

Duchbat (Dutch Battalion) The Dutch peacekeepers under the command of the UNPROFOR stationed in Potočari.

Džezva A coffee pot.

Fildžan A handleless coffee cup.

General Philippe Morillon Commanded the United Nations Forces in Bosnia (1992–1993)

Hodža Imam in Bosnian

ICTY (International Criminal Tribunal for the Former Yugoslavia) The Appeals Chamber ruled in 2004 that the Srebrenica massacre constituted genocide, making it the first genocide conviction in Europe since the Holocaust.

Lieux de mémoire (Sites of memory) A concept introduced by Nora to describe sites where memory crystallises and persists. Srebrenica transformed into a *lieu de mémoire*—a symbol of trauma and international failure—after the genocide.

Mama Mother.

Mejtef Religious classes at the Mosque, typically attended once a week by village refugees.

Memoricide The systematic obliteration of archives and cultural heritage (such as libraries, mosques, and museums) to destroy the legacy and memory of Bosnian history.

Milieu de mémoire (Real environments of memory) A concept describing environments where memory was lived, organically maintained by the people and their interactions, such as Srebrenica before the war.

Mosquitoes A disparaging name used for sporting or farming planes that Serbs had equipped with machine guns and bombs.

Mujahideen Is the plural form of *Mujahid*, meaning someone who fights for Islam — typically in a religious or ideological struggle, often interpreted as 'holy warriors

Nana Grandmother.

Naser Orić Bosnian Commander of the Army of the Republic of Bosnia and Herzegovina (ARBiH) forces in Srebrenica.

Potočari The site of the UN Protection Force (UNPROFOR) base near Srebrenica. The Srebrenica-Potočari Memorial and Cemetery is located here.

Rakija A traditional Balkan fruit brandy, often homemade plum brandy. It was used by residents during the siege as a form of recreation, a pain reliever, and a means to "cheat hunger".

Ratko Mladić Serb Commander. He led the campaign to drive Muslims from eastern Bosnia and forced Muslim leaders to capitulate.

Republika Srpska (Serb Republic) The entity declared by Bosnian Serb nationalists; Srebrenica is now under its administration and controls the narrative.

Safe Zone Srebrenica was declared a UN-protected safe zone on April 16, 1993, a designation that proved to be an illusion as Serbs encircled the enclave, attempting to starve the population.

Šamija Headscarf.

Srpsko-Hrvatski Serbo-Croat language, which was taught in schools and underlined the marginalisation of Bosnian culture and identity.

Tito's era Refers to the period when Josip Broz Tito ruled Yugoslavia, from the end of World War II in 1945 until his death in 1980.

Torbari The name given to refugees or troops who looted, meaning "bag-carriers".

UNPROFOR (United Nations Protection Force) The UN peacekeepers, including the Dutchbat, stationed at Potočari.

Zadruga A patriarchal system under which "material goods were communally held by the patrilineage".

Seka Torlak Series

Forged on the war-torn streets of Srebrenica, Seka Torlak fights for justice, retribution and truth.

0.5: The Tree That Stood Still

Srebrenica 1992

In a town shattered by prejudice, two girls forge a friendship that defies the ravages of war...

Seka and Zora have been inseparable, growing up as neighbours and best friends in the once peaceful town of Srebrenica. But as Yugoslavia begins to splinter and nationalism sweeps through the region, their town is torn apart by prejudice and violence. Suddenly, Seka and Zora find themselves on opposite sides of a brutal conflict, their friendship strained by the rising tide of hatred.

As the horrors of war descend upon Srebrenica, Seka and Zora's bond is tested like never before. With nationalist propaganda fuelling distrust and fear, the streets they once played in become battlegrounds.

Amidst the chaos, they must navigate a world where friends can become enemies overnight. Will their friendship endure the storm of war and prejudice, or will it be shattered by the forces tearing their town apart?

Book 1: Time Kneels Between Mountains
Srebrenica, 1992
In a town where survival is a daily battle, there are those who seek justice...

Overnight, Seka Torlak's life as a regular teenager is upended as Srebrenica, her once peaceful town, falls under siege and she faces starvation, shelling, and sniper attacks. When desperately needed antibiotics and food disappear and are sold on the black market, Seka vows to investigate the corruption and bring the culprits to justice.

As the war ravages Srebrenica, Seka's resilience is tested as she navigates loss, fear, and the harsh realities of war. Yet, amidst the devastation, she finds a glimmer of hope as her relationship with Ramo blossoms from friendship to love. But as she fights for justice and love, will Seka triumph, or will the brutal war tear everything she holds dear apart?

Bonus Short Story: Belma's Liberation
In a village shadowed by abuse, there are those with courage who fight for liberation...

Sign up to my newsletter and read *Belma's Liberation* to find out how Seka saved her from her abusive father

Book 2: Ghosts Among the Gumtrees

Melbourne, 1997

In a city where the guilty roam free, there are those who seek retribution...

After surviving the brutal siege of Srebrenica, Seka Torlak is trying to rebuild her life as a refugee in Melbourne, 1997. But her fragile peace is shattered when she spots a war criminal responsible for her father's death walking freely in the city. Determined to uncover his true identity and bring him to justice, Seka delves into an investigation that reveals a sinister underbelly of suburbia, where genocide deniers hide in plain sight.

Haunted by memories of war and loss, Seka grapples with the raging conflict within her: the pursuit of justice versus the thirst for retribution. As she navigates this perilous path, she must decide what she is willing to sacrifice for the truth. Will Seka find her salvation, or will she lose her soul in the process?

Bonus Short Story: Zora's Story

In the ruins of war, there are those who cling to memories of friendship...

Sign up to my newsletter and read *Zora's Story* to find out her story in escaping the war.

Book 3: Mad Dawn Winter

Riverwood, 1998

In a town submerged with secrets and corruption, there are those who seek the truth...

Seka Torlak, now a journalism cadet, relocates to the tranquil town of Riverwood in 1998, seeking a fresh start. However, her peace is short-lived when she stumbles upon a cold case involving the murder of a former Vietnam Vet. Driven by a grieving mother's plea for justice, Seka begins to uncover a web of secrets that this seemingly idyllic town has buried deep.

In her quest for truth, Seka befriends Dawn Winter, a fellow Bosnian woman haunted by the loss of a friend and ostracised by the townspeople for her tributes to the fallen. As Seka digs deeper, she finds herself entangled in a dangerous game of deceit and loyalty, facing ghosts of the past and present. Will she unravel the truth and deliver justice before it's too late, or will the town's dark secrets consume her?

Bonus Short Story: Art's War

In a time of loss and grief, there are those who pursue the truth...

Sign up to my newsletter and read *Art's Fall* to find out about his investigation first-hand.

Bonus Short Story: The Regrets of Ben Hayes

In a war where fear reigns, love remains unspoken...

Sign up to my newsletter and read *The Regrets of Ben Hayes* to find out about his first love during his service as a National Serviceman.

About the author

Amra Pajalic is an award-winning Australian author, educator, and indie publisher known for crafting compelling stories that blend heart, humour, and heritage. Her work explores themes of identity, belonging, and resilience, often drawing from her Bosnian background.

She won the 2009 Melbourne Prize for Literature's Civic Choice Award for her debut novel *The Good Daughter*, re-released as *Sabiha's Dilemma* (Pishukin Press, 2022). The anthology she co-edited, *Growing up Muslim in Australia* (Allen and Unwin, 2014), was shortlisted for the 2015 Children's Book Council of the year awards and her memoir *Things Nobody Knows But Me* (Transit Lounge, 2019) was shortlisted for the 2020 National Biography Award. Her short story collection The Cuckoo's Song (Pishukin Press) features previously published and prize-winning stories.

Amra is the author of the Sassy Saints series, a young adult contemporary trilogy set in Melbourne's western suburbs. These stories feature smart-mouthed teens, love triangles, fake friends, and fierce girl power, offering a refreshing take on multicultural Australian life.

She is also the creator of the gripping Seka Torlak crime mystery series. Forged on the war-torn streets of Srebrenica, Seka Torlak fights for justice, retribution and truth.

Amra is committed to accessibility and inclusion in publishing. Through her micro-press, Pishukin Press, she releases her titles in a wide range of formats—including audiobook, large print, dyslexic font, paperback, ebook, and hardback—to ensure all readers can experience her stories.

Amra Pajalić publishes her dark fiction using pen name A. P. Pajalic. She also publishes romance novels under pen name Mae Archer.

- goodreads.com/author/show/3310015.Amra_Pajalic
- facebook.com/AmraPajalicAuthor/
- instagram.com/amrapajalicauthor/
- https://twitter.com/AmraPajalic
- tiktok.com/@amrapajalic
- youtube.com/c/AmraPajalicAuthor

SIGN UP FOR AMRA'S AUTHOR NEWSLETTER

For news, giveaways, bonus material, and sneak peeks, please sign up to her newsletter below.

www.amrapajalic.com

Also by

Seka Torlak Series
The Tree That Stood Still
Time Kneels Between Mountains
Ghosts Among the Gumtrees
Mad Dawn Winter

Memoir
Things Nobody Knows But Me
Growing up Muslim in Australia

Sassy Saints Series
Sabiha's Dilemma
Alma's Loyalty
Jesse's Triumph

Young Adult
The Cuckoo's Song
The Climb

Romance as Mae Archer
Return to Me
Hollywood Dreams

Vintage Dreams

Dark Fiction/Horror as A.P. Pajalic
Woman on the Edge

www.ingramcontent.com/pod-product-compliance
Lightning Source LLC
Chambersburg PA
CBHW060453080526
44584CB00015B/1426